W9-CAX-509

This book is presented to

Karli

It was given to you by

Grandma

Date

1/10/16

# 365 Bible Promises

## for Little Hearts

A new Bible promise for each day of the year

## Phil A. Smouse

BARBOUR
PUBLISHING

© 2009 by Phil A. Smouse

Print ISBN 978-1-61626-680-6

eBook Editions:
Adobe Digital Edition (.epub) 978-1-60742-492-5
Kindle and MobiPocket Edition (.prc) 978-1-60742-493-2

All rights reserved. No part of this publication may be reproduced or transmitted for commercial purposes, except for brief quotations in printed reviews, without written permission of the publisher.

Churches and other noncommercial interests may reproduce portions of this book without the express written permission of Barbour Publishing, provided that the text does not exceed 500 words and that the text is not material quoted from another publisher. When reproducing text from this book, include the following credit line: "From *My Everyday Promise Bible*, published by Barbour Publishing, Inc. Used by permission."

Elements of the readings on days 159, 182, and 229 have been adapted from *My Utmost for His Highest* by Oswald Chambers.

All scripture verses have been paraphrased by the author.

Published by Barbour Publishing, Inc., P.O. Box 719, Uhrichsville, Ohio 44683, www.barbourbooks.com

*Our mission is to publish and distribute inspirational products offering exceptional value and biblical encouragement to the masses.*

ecpa Member of the
Evangelical Christian
Publishers Association

Printed in the United States of America.
Versa Press, Inc., East Peoria, IL 61611; January 2012; D10003108

*Heaven and earth will pass away,*
*but My Word will last forever.*

MATTHEW 24:35

For Annette Rose,
whose tender heart is teaching me to be more like Jesus,
for O. C., whose life and words continue to challenge and inspire,
and for P. M., whose trust and constant encouragement
make everything easy.

# A NOTE to PARENTS

*The grass withers and the flowers fall,
but the Word of our God stands forever.*

ISAIAH 40:8

The answer to every need we face can be found in God's Word—if we take time to look for it! *365 Bible Promises for Little Hearts* will encourage your children to search God's Word for answers to all the big and little questions they face each day.

I've collected a year's worth of favorite Bible promises and put them at your child's fingertips in a language they can understand—and in a format that will make the time they spend in God's Word a joy and delight. They may even fall in love with Jesus along the way. That is truly my heart's desire.

Phil A. Smouse
January 2012

# I WILL NEVER LEAVE YOU

*I will never leave you
or take My love away.*

JOSHUA 1:5

Jesus loves you just the way you are. He will never leave you. He will never stop loving you. Nothing will *ever* make Him take His love away. God is real. His love is *forever*. And it is here to stay.

# Gentle Words

*Gentle words
turn anger into kindness.*

### Proverbs 15:1

Anger is like a fire. The more you feed it, the bigger it grows. But kind words are like a river of cool water. Speak them with love and the fire of anger goes out.

# GOOD THINGS!

*A man who loves to give
good things to others will be
showered with blessings from the Lord.*

PROVERBS 22:9

Jesus is happy when we help each other.
Do you like to do good things for other people?
Then you will see God do good things for *you!*

# WITH ALL YOUR HEART

*Trust the LORD with all your heart,
and He will show you
the right thing to do.*

PROVERBS 3:5–6

Did you ever need help with a big decision? Some decisions are easy. And some are not! But when you ask God for help—*and trust that it will come*—He will show you the right thing to do every time.

# MUCH BETTER!

*A happy heart
makes everyone feel better.*

PROVERBS 17:22

Do you know people who are feeling blue? Would you like to help them feel better? Your happy heart is just what they need. Take time to do something special and watch what God will do!

# ALL THINGS ARE POSSIBLE

*With God all things are possible.*

MATTHEW 19:26

God's Word is the truth. When He says something you can believe it. And His Word says, *with God all things are possible.*

# YOUR HEART'S DESIRE

*Make your friendship with God
the most important thing in your life
and He will give you your heart's desire.*

PSALM 37:4

If you could have *anything*, what would you want? The Bible says when you give your heart to Jesus, then live in a way that is pleasing to Him, God will gladly give you your heart's desire!

# DON'T WORRY!

*Give all your cares to Jesus
because He cares for you.*

1 PETER 5:7

Worry is like a heavy weight. You'll get hurt
if you try to carry it alone. So what should you do
with it? *Give it to Jesus!* His arms are strong. Let
Him pick up your worries and carry them away.

# LET THERE BE LIGHT

*Your word is the lamp that lights the road ahead to show me the way to go.*

PSALM 119:105

Have you ever been afraid of the dark? Yes, it can be scary. But you must always remember this: darkness has no power over light. When the lights come on, darkness goes—*instantly!* There's never a fight. Light wins every time.

# I Love You, Too

*Come near to God
and He will come near to you.*

James 4:8

When you love someone very much you want to be close to them, don't you? Do you love Jesus? Then talk to Him today. Tell Him how you feel. Open up your heart. Let His love pour in.

# HIDE AND SEEK

*You will seek me and find me
when you search with all your heart.*

JEREMIAH 29:13

Do you like to play hide-and-seek? It's fun
to hide. But it's more fun to be found, isn't it?
Jesus is easy to find. *He isn't hiding!* He's waiting
for you right now with His arms open wide.

# SEEDS OF PEACE

*All who plant the seeds of peace will
grow a garden that is pleasing to God.*

JAMES 3:18

What kind of seeds are you planting? Do
you want a beautiful garden of peace and joy?
Of course! Then you must remember to plant
kindness, patience, *forgiveness,* and love.

# A HEART AT PEACE

*A heart at peace
brings happiness and joy.*

PROVERBS 14:30

The peace Jesus gives brings life and joy. Are anger, worry, fear, and doubt knocking on the door of your heart? *Don't let them in!* Your heart belongs to Jesus. There's no room left for anything else.

# NOW AND THEN

*A man's anger does not bring about the good and godly life our Lord desires.*

JAMES 1:20

Everyone gets mad now and then. There's nothing wrong with that. But when you get angry about *everything* all the time, it's a warning sign. Something is wrong and you need to change.

# I WILL ANSWER

*When you call upon me
I will answer you.*

PSALM 91:15

Jesus hears you when you pray. You don't need fancy words or made-up sayings. Jesus wants to talk to *you!* So tell Him what you want. Tell Him what you need. He will listen. *He will answer.* Jesus loves you. You can talk to Him right now.

# TRUE FRIENDS

*A friend loves at all times.*

PROVERBS 17:17

Do you have a friend? Then you have a great treasure. True friends love each other no matter what. They know how easy it is to make a mistake. And they know how good it feels to hear, "That's okay, I forgive you. You'll always be my friend."

# NICE AND EASY

*The Lord is not slow
in keeping His promises.*

2 PETER 3:9

God is not in a hurry. Not today. Not tomorrow. *Not ever!* So there's no need for you to be, either. God knows what you need. And when the time is just right, His answer will come.

# THAT'S A LONG TIME

*To God one day is the same as
a thousand years, and a thousand
years are the same as one day.*

2 PETER 3:8

Do you like to wait? Does it seem like a
thousand years have gone by since you asked
God for that one special thing? Cheer up! And
hang on. The answer may very well come today.

# Everyone I Love

*I correct and discipline
everyone I love.*

## Revelation 3:19

It's never fun to be corrected. But Jesus loves you too much to let you run very far away. Are you running now? More than anything in the world, Jesus wants you to come back home.

# THE BREAD OF LIFE

*I am the bread of life. If you come to me you will never go hungry.*

JOHN 6:35

Your body is amazing. But it can't last long without food. Your Spirit needs food, as well. What kind? *The Jesus kind!* He is the bread your Spirit needs to come alive. Spend time talking to Him as you hide His Word deep down in your heart.

# WALK BY FAITH

*We walk by faith and not by sight.*

2 CORINTHIANS 5:7

**What** does it mean to walk by faith?
It means you trust God's Word and do what
it says—even if everything and everyone
around you tells you it cannot be true.

# BLESSED

*God has blessed His people.*
*No one can ever change that.*

NUMBERS 23:20

Has anyone ever tried to tell you you're no good or that nothing good will ever happen to you? *That is a lie.* God's Word says you are blessed. And no one can ever take His blessing away.

# Wonderful Power

*The heartfelt prayers of a godly man have great power and bring wonderful results.*

James 5:16

Your prayers are powerful. When you are living in a way that is pleasing to God, you can ask God for *any good thing*. He will move heaven and earth to share His *best* with the ones He loves.

# Don't Give Up

*Never get tired of doing good. When the time is right you will be rewarded if you don't give up.*

GALATIANS 6:9

Are you tired, worn out, and ready to quit? It's not always easy to do good. Sometimes it isn't any fun. But it *is* always right. *So don't give up!* God will do something *amazing* if you don't give up.

# That's a Big One

*Do not point out where others
are wrong unless you want them
to do the same thing to you.*

MATTHEW 7:1

It's easy to see each other's faults. But it takes
a true friend to look past those problems and
love the way Jesus loves—without finding fault
or trying to fix others in any way at all.

# WISE WORDS

*The words of the wise
bring healing.*

PROVERBS 12:18

Careless, unkind, angry words can be as painful as a sword to the heart. But the right words spoken at the right time—*from a pure heart*—bring forgiveness, healing, and joy.

# More Than Enough

*A man who works hard
will always have more than enough.*

Proverbs 12:11

Hands that work hard are a blessing to every-one. Do you have a warm bed and a full tummy? Someone worked hard to get those things for you. Why not thank God for that hard worker today?

# WHAT A DAY

*I will see God with my very own eyes.*
*Oh, how I wish that day would come!*

JOB 19:27

Do you ever wish you could see Jesus face-to-face? Wouldn't you love to sit beside Him and pour out your heart? One day you will. It may take a long time. It may not. But that day will come. And oh, what a day it will be!

# JUST ASK

*You do not have
because you do not ask.*

JAMES 4:2

Jesus will give you *everything* you need.
What good thing do you need today?
Jesus knows where it is. He's ready to
give it to you. All you have to do is ask.

# Just Awhile Longer

*Don't get upset if things seem
to go wrong. When faith is tested,
patience has a chance to grow.*

James 1:2–3

Have you been waiting long for an answer to
your prayers? Don't get upset. Let your heart be
filled with joy! When you learn to wait without
worry or fear, God's answer is never too far away.

# ON THE ROCK

*All who hear My words and do them
are like a wise man who built
a strong house on solid rock.*

MATTHEW 7:24

Life without God is like a sand castle. It can look beautiful. But a tiny bit of water can wash it all away. A wise man builds his house on the rock of God's Word. Storms may come. But his house is strong. It can never be washed away.

# It's Covered

*True love covers a mountain of sins.*

1 Peter 4:8

When love sees the sins of others, what does it do? Does it point an angry finger? Does it turn and walk away? *No! Love looks in the mirror.* It sees a person who makes a mountain of mistakes, too. So *love forgives* and does its best to be a friend.

# WHAT DO YOU NEED?

*God will take care of all your needs
with the wonderful riches
that belong to Jesus.*

PHILIPPIANS 4:19

Jesus has everything you need to live and
be happy. When you truly *need* something,
He will make sure you have it. There is
*nothing* too big or too hard for God!

# GOOD WORK

*Be strong. Don't give up.*
*Your work will be rewarded.*

2 CHRONICLES 15:7

It's not always easy to do the right thing. Some days it's just about impossible. But don't give up. There is a day when God's answer will come. He will reward the good work you've done.

# WAY TO GO!

*I will teach you and show you
the right way to go.*

PSALM 32:8

The Bible is the key to the most amazing
treasure you will ever find. It will unlock
a door that leads straight to God's heart!

# TRUST GOD AND WORK

*The plans of those who trust God and work hard will prosper and be blessed.*

PROVERBS 21:5

When you trust God and work hard, you will always have enough. But when you are in a big hurry to get your work done, you will wind up in need very *quickly* indeed!

# REAL TREASURE

*Godliness with a happy heart
is a very great treasure.*

1 TIMOTHY 6:6

When you fall in love with money and things your heart becomes like a glass with no bottom. The more you try to fill it, the emptier it gets. Real treasure is found on the *inside*—in your heart. Nothing can ever take that gift away.

# FREE AT LAST

*If the Son sets you free,
you are truly free.*

JOHN 8:36

Does Jesus live inside your heart? Then you are truly free! Every good thing God has belongs to you. The past doesn't matter. You are forgiven. Jesus loves you. You are *free*.

# NOTHING!

*Nothing can separate us
from the love of God.*

ROMANS 8:39

What can separate you from the love of God?
*Nothing!* Not what happened yesterday—not what
will happen tomorrow. Nothing up high. Nothing
down below. Nothing. No one. *Not even death!*
Nothing can separate you from the love of God.

# FEAR NOT

*God did not give us a spirit of fear.*

2 TIMOTHY 1:7

Jesus loves you. He knows how you feel. You don't have to worry. There's no reason to be afraid. Jesus is bigger than every problem you face. He will work things out for your good. You can trust Him with all of your heart.

# CLEAN AND GREEN

*He filled us with power, love,
and self-control.*

2 TIMOTHY 1:7

Jesus planted a beautiful garden in your heart.
He filled it with courage, strength, peace, and joy.
Have you been anxious, worried, nervous, or upset?
Those feelings are like weeds. They did not come
from Jesus. Pull them out before they can grow.

# THAT'S GOOD NEWS

*A godly man is not afraid of bad news.
His heart is filled with courage
for he trusts in the Lord.*

PSALM 112:7

Jesus is happy when we trust Him. It fills His heart with unspeakable joy. Our courage shows Jesus we believe His *good news,* no matter what anyone else says.

# JUST FOR YOU

*His banner over me is love.*

SONG OF SOLOMON 2:4

Do you like to put up decorations on special days? They make everything beautiful, don't they? Did you know Jesus loves you so much He decorates *every day?* But not just with banners or streamers or lights. The banner Jesus uses for someone as special as you is *God's love!*

# READY TO CHANGE

*Your sins have
cut you off from God.*

ISAIAH 59:2

Did you ever want to do something you knew
was wrong, but you decided to do it anyway?
God calls that *sin.* Sin breaks God's heart. But
that's not all. Sin forces God to hide His face
from you until you decide you're ready to change.

# DAY 45

# WHO, ME?

*All have sinned and fall short of the good and godly life the Lord desires.*

ROMANS 3:23

Have you ever sinned? You're not alone! God says *everyone* has sinned. And He should know. But here's the good news: *God will forgive you!* If you tell Him you're sorry, He will wash away your sins and help your heart to become like His.

# Pure Joy

*If you confess your sins, God will forgive your sins and you will be clean and pure again.*

1 John 1:9

Jesus loves you. He is not angry. He wants to forgive *and He will*. Did you tell Him you're sorry for the things you've done wrong? Then the past is gone. He won't ever bring it up again. You can start over. *You are forgiven*. All things are new!

# JOHN 3:16

*God loved the world so much He gave His one and only Son so all who believe in Him will never die, but will live with God in heaven forever.*

JOHN 3:16

How much does God love you? He loves you so much He sent His one and only Son to die on the cross to take your sins away.

# Punish Me Instead

*The blood of Jesus
washes away all of our sins.*

1 John 1:7

Jesus never, ever sinned. But you and I have. And the punishment for sin is death. Why didn't God punish us for our sin? Because Jesus spread out His arms and said, *"Punish me instead!"*

# ALL THINGS ARE NEW!

*Anyone who belongs to Jesus has become a new person. The old life is gone. A new life has begun!*

2 CORINTHIANS 5:17

When you give your heart to Jesus, you become a new person. Not on the outside—*on the inside.* Sin moves out and Jesus moves in. And when Jesus moves in, He makes *all things* brand new.

# JOY AND DELIGHT

*Blessed is the man who does not follow the advice of the wicked or walk down paths made by sinful men.*

PSALM 1:1

The path Jesus walks is a joy and delight. It's filled with wonderful, beautiful things. When your hand is in His, you will stay on that path. And all the good things that are His will be yours.

# PLANTED BY THE WATER

*The godly man is like a tree planted by the water. Its leaves do not wither. Its fruit is delicious. Everything he does will prosper.*

PSALM 1:3

God's Word is the water your heart needs to grow. When your roots go down deep into His River of Life, you will grow taller, stronger, and more like Jesus every day.

# PRIDE AND JOY

*The Lord delights
in those who love Him.*

PSALM 147:11

**What** makes Jesus happy? Do you know?
I'll give you a hint. It's something very close.
In fact it's here in this room. The gift that fills
His heart with joy is something very special—*you!*

# YES AND AMEN

*Because of Jesus all God's
promises end in yes and Amen.*

2 CORINTHIANS 1:20

God's Word is full of amazing promises.
Will God keep those promises? Because of
what Jesus did on the cross the answer is "*yes.*"
So you can jump and shout "*Amen!*"

# WHAT DO YOU THINK?

*The way you think on the inside
is clearly seen by the way you
behave on the outside.*

PROVERBS 23:7

The things we do can tell others a lot about
who we really are. Does your heart belong to
Jesus? Then everything you do will leave behind
the wonderful smell of God's beauty and love.

# ONE OF THOSE DAYS

*In this world you will have trouble.*
*But be of good cheer.*
*I have overcome the world.*

JOHN 16:33

Some days *everything* seems to go wrong. Does that mean God is mad at you? Of course not. This world is not your *forever* home. None of us will ever truly be happy until we're safe and warm in our real home—*heaven*—with Jesus.

# HOME AGAIN

*Our real home is in heaven.*

PHILIPPIANS 3:20

**What** will heaven be like? Does anyone know? I'm not really sure. But I can tell you this: One day Jesus will change your earthly body into a heavenly one like His own. And you will see Him face-to-face.

# THIS IS FOR YOU

*Good will come to the person who gives generously to those in need.*

PSALM 112:5

People who love money never have enough. But people who love to give to others always have everything they need and more.

# SWEET SLEEP

*When you lie down you will not
be afraid. Your sleep will be sweet.*

PROVERBS 3:24

Why are you tossing and turning again?
Is your heart troubled? *Shhhh...* Be still. God
is here. Give your cares to Jesus. Wrap yourself
in His arms and let Him wash your fears away.

# My Weakness

*When I am weak,
then I am strong.*

2 Corinthians 12:10

There is nothing wrong with being weak. Weak people know when they need help. Don't *ever* be afraid to ask God for help. His mighty arms have all the strength you will ever need.

# MEEK AND MILD

*The meek will inherit the earth
and enjoy great peace.*

PSALM 37:11

Are you humble, gentle, loving, and kind?
One day the whole earth and everything in it
will belong to you!

# COMPLETELY HIS

*God's kindness teaches us to turn
from our sins and give our hearts
completely to Him.*

ROMANS 2:4

Jesus knows everything about you. He knows
about the good things. He knows about the bad
things, too. You don't have to pretend there are
no bad things. Jesus is not angry. He wants to
help you. Won't you please give Him your heart?

# Joy!

*The joy of the LORD is your strength*

NEHEMIAH 8:10

Where does your joy come from? Does it come from the people and things around you? If so, you will be happy one day and grumpy the next. But when your joy comes from Jesus, you can find a way to be happy even when people and things make you want to scream.

# WONDERFUL

*A good name is better
than fine perfume.*

ECCLESIASTES 7:1

Some things smell *wonderful*. And some do not! The things you say and do can be like the sweet smell of a favorite perfume. Or they can tell everyone you meet that you really need to take a bath.

# WELL DONE

*Finishing well is better
than beginning well.*

ECCLESIASTES 7:8

Getting started is easy. Just about anyone
can do that. But it takes God's help to do
God's work God's way—and to finish that
work in a way that is pleasing to Him.

# I Heard That

*The LORD is near to everyone who calls upon His name with a sincere heart.*

PSALM 145:18

You can tell Jesus exactly how you feel. You don't need to promise Him anything. You don't need to try to make a deal. Jesus knows your heart. He hears you when you pray. Why don't you take some time and talk to Him today?

# EVERLASTING LOVE

*I love you with a love
that lasts forever.*

JEREMIAH 31:3

Jesus has always loved you. Before the world began He knew you by name. Nothing *anyone* can do will ever take away God's love. His love for you will last *forever*.

# I PROMISE

*The Lord will keep all of His promises.*

PSALM 145:13

Are you having a bad day? Sometimes it seems like God's promises will *never* come true. *But that is a lie.* Don't *ever* sit down on that patch of thorns. Stand tall on God's promises and give Him thanks!

# THE WAY OUT

*When you are tempted to sin,*
*God will show you the way out.*

1 CORINTHIANS 10:13

Did you ever want to do something wrong?
That's what it means to be tempted. Jesus knows
those feelings will come. That doesn't make you
a bad person. If you ask for help, God will show
you the way out. *But it's up to you to take it.*

# THAT'S A SILLY QUESTION

*You don't need to be afraid. Every hair on your head is numbered. God loves you more than anything in the world.*

LUKE 12:7

Can I ask you a silly question? Did you ever try to count your hair? God has! If He cares about something as small as that, what will you ever need that He would forget to provide?

# SILVER AND GOLD

*A man who finds wisdom
will be filled with joy. For wisdom
is more valuable than silver or gold.*

PROVERBS 3:13–14

Did you ever want something very much? When you finally got it, what happened? Was it all you hoped for? Or did it cause more problems than it solved? That's no surprise. The only real treasure in this silly world is a heart filled with God's love.

# HE KNOWS MY NAME

*Fear not. Your sins have been forgiven.*
*I have called you by name.*
*You are mine.*

ISAIAH 43:1

Long before the world began—before anything
was or ever would be—Jesus knew you by name.
His heart cried out, "I love you. *You are beautiful.*
You will always be mine."

# LET THERE BE LIGHT

*You are my lamp O LORD.*
*You turn my darkness into light.*

2 SAMUEL 22:29

Darkness cannot live for *one second* when there is light. Are you in the dark just now? *Then let there be light!* Flood your heart and mind with God's Word and the darkness will disappear.

# GOODNESS AND MERCY

*Goodness and mercy will
follow me all the days of my life.*

PSALM 23:6

Did you ever get the feeling you were being
followed? Well don't look now. . .*but you are!*
You might as well get used to it. God's goodness
and loving kindness are going to follow you
*everywhere*—all the days of your life!

# HERE THEY COME

*All these blessings will chase after you and catch you when you obey the voice of the Lord.*

DEUTERONOMY 28:2

What happens when you do what God says? *You will be blessed!* How blessed? God's Word says you will be blessed in the city, blessed in the country, blessed in your body, blessed in your work, blessed with the things you need, blessed when you come in, and blessed when you go out!

# I'll Do It!

*If you obey the commandments of the
Lord and take care to do what He says,
God will bless the things you do.*

DEUTERONOMY 28:12–13

When God says something, you can believe
it! And God says when you listen to His voice
and then do what He says, you will be *blessed*—
every good thing He has will be yours as well.

# DO YOU SEE WHAT I SEE?

*Keep your eyes on Jesus, who saw the joy new life would bring and gladly went to the cross to take our sins away.*

HEBREWS 12:2

Whose eyes are you looking through? What do you see? Everyone wants to give up now and then. But when you look at things through Jesus' eyes, you will be able to see the happy ending that's coming soon—if you don't give up.

# TRUST HIM!

*Be strong in the Lord and
trust in His mighty power.*

EPHESIANS 6:10

Every word God says is true. You don't ever
have to be afraid. So trust Him. Trust His Word.
Risk *everything* and watch what He will do!

# I FORGIVE YOU

*God's anger lasts only for a moment.*
*But His favor lasts a lifetime.*

PSALM 30:5

Sin breaks God's heart. Will it make
Him turn His back on you? *Of course not!*
When you tell God you're sorry and then
do your best to change, He will forgive you
and wrap you in His arms again.

# BE STILL AND KNOW

*Be still and know that I am God.*

PSALM 46:10

Shhh. . . Do you like the quiet? Silence makes some people very nervous. *But that's where Jesus lives.* God's voice is still and small. He won't shout to be heard. You must be quiet *on the inside* if you want to hear Him.

# RIGHT AT HOME

*Everyone who calls on the name
of the Lord will be saved.*

ROMANS 10:13

How do you get Jesus to live inside your heart?
*Just ask!* It doesn't matter what you've done.
When you open up the door to your heart, Jesus
will come inside and make Himself right at home.

# NOT GUILTY

*There is no longer any punishment waiting for those whose hearts belong to Jesus.*

ROMANS 8:1

Does Jesus live inside your heart? Then you are forgiven! Your sins are gone. *Forgotten!* God won't ever—*ever*—bring them up again.

# THE BEST

*Whoever thinks he is the best will be humbled, and whoever humbles himself will be the best.*

MATTHEW 23:12

Do you want to be the biggest and the best? *Watch out!* If you puff your head up too much it just might pop! Jesus says the very best way to stand tall is to get down on your knees.

# LIVING IN GOD'S LIGHT

*When you love your brother
you live in God's light, and your life
will help others to stand and not fall.*

1 JOHN 2:10

Your friend needs the light Jesus put in your
heart. When you love others, God's beauty will
shine like the sun. They will know *for sure* that
God is alive and His love is for real!

# ENOUGH

*The man who loves money
never has enough.*

ECCLESIASTES 5:10

How much is enough? When a man loves money he will say, "Just a little bit more than I have." But when a man loves *Jesus* he will say, "I already have everything I will ever need."

# OOPS!

*An angry man does foolish things.*
*But the gift of a godly man is wisdom.*

PROVERBS 14:17–18

Do you know how to make a big mistake?
It's easy. Just do something your heart knows is
wrong. Do you know how to fix a big mistake?
That's easy, too. *Learn to say, "I'm sorry!"*

# AN EASY ONE

*When you pray you will have
what you ask for—if you believe.*

MATTHEW 21:22

Jesus hears you when you pray. The answer
for everything you will ever need is already in His
hands. Nothing is too hard for Him—*nothing!*
Trust God today and watch what He will do!

# Running Over

*Give and it will be given to you.*

LUKE 6:38

When you give freely and with joy, Jesus will move the hearts and hands of those around you to give back—so much you won't have enough room to take it all in!

# I Love You, Too

*The way you treat others
is the way they will treat you.*

LUKE 6:38

Jesus is happy when we love each other.
Do you treat your friends with kindness?
Do you think about the way your words and
deeds make them feel? Then God will make
sure they do the very same thing for you!

# I Needed That

*My grace is all you really need.*
*My power flows freely—with nothing*
*in the way—when you are weak.*

2 Corinthians 12:9

There is nothing wrong with needing help. A humble heart is the key that unlocks the door and allows God's incredible power and love to flood your life with every good thing.

# WHO, ME?

*You are the light of the world.*

MATTHEW 5:14

Yes, YOU are the light of the world. . .
*So shine your light!* Let everything you say and
do shine with His beauty for everyone to see!

# SWEET FEET

*How beautiful are the feet of those
who bring good news!*

ISAIAH 52:7

**What** a wonderful thing it is to welcome
a friend bearing good news! You *are* that friend
every time you share God's love with others.

# Rest

*Come to Me,
and I will give you rest.*

MATTHEW 11:28

Have you been working very hard? Do you feel like you've been carrying your stuff *and* the stuff of everyone around you? If you will lay it all down and come to Jesus, He will give you the rest you need.

# THE SECRET PLACE

*When you make your home
in the Secret Place with God, you will
find rest in the shadow of His wings.*

PSALM 91:1

What is the Secret Place? It's not a place at all!
It's the *time* you give completely to Jesus. The
Secret Place is a lot like a *nest* where you can
snuggle up in the warmth and safety of your
Daddy's arms and share your heart with Him.

# DADDY

*Now we call Him, "Abba, Father."*
*For His spirit joins with our spirit to*
*let us know that we are His children.*

ROMANS 8:15–16

*Abba* is a Bible word that means, "Daddy." When Jesus comes to live inside your heart, you become His child—and you can call Him *Daddy!*

# THE WAY TO GO

*"Abba, Father,"* Jesus cried out,
*"All things are possible for you."*

MARK 14:36

What does Jesus want? He wants your heart.
Are you facing a big decision? There is *nothing*
God cannot do. Let your Daddy show you the
right way to go.

# VERY GOOD

*God saw everything He made
and it was very good.*

GENESIS 1:31

Are your ears too big? Is your nose too long?
Do you smell funny? God was not having a bad
day when he made you. You are *perfect* just the way
you are—and He loves you more than anything.

# WONDERFULLY WELL

*You created every part of me.*
*Your work is wonderful.*
*I know that very well!*

PSALM 139:13–14

You are not a mistake. You are not an accident. God made you with His very own hands. Before you were born, He knew your name. Everything about you is absolutely beautiful—just the way He always wanted it to be!

# DELIGHTFUL

*The LORD your God is with you. . .*
*You are His great delight.*

ZEPHANIAH 3:17

Jesus loves you with all of His heart. You are His precious treasure—His joy and delight. He wants to be with you more than words can say.

# MIGHTY TO SAVE

*The LORD your God is with you. . .*
*He is mighty to save.*

ZEPHANIAH 3:17

Jesus made the world and everything in it.
No mountain is too big for Him to push aside.
When you call on His name, God will move
heaven and earth to come to your rescue.

# SING FOR JOY

*The LORD your God is with you. . .*
*He will sing for joy because of you.*

ZEPHANIAH 3:17

Did you know that God likes to sing?
It's true! *Listen. . .* Can you hear Him? God
is with you right now. He made up a special
love song, and He's singing it just for you!

# SHHHHH!

*The LORD your God is with you. . .*
*He will quiet you with His love.*

ZEPHANIAH 3:17

Worry is a lot like noise. It spreads out fast and covers *everything*. Soon you can't hear anything else! Are you worried today? Jesus loves you. He knows what you need. Let Him wrap His arms around you and quiet you with His love.

# EVERYTHING YOU NEED

*God's power gives us everything
we need to live a godly life.*

2 PETER 1:3

Learning to follow Jesus is a lot like learning to ride a bike. It's not easy at first, and you fall down a lot! But that doesn't mean you have to give up. God's promises give you everything you need to get up, try again, and *get it right!*

# I PROMISE

*God gave us these great and precious promises so we can escape the evil in this world and learn to be more like Him.*

2 PETER 1:4

God's promises are like a well with no bottom. You can take as much as you need, *whenever you need it, as often as you need it*—and the well will never run dry!

# COURAGE!

*Be strong. Be brave.*
*Wait for the LORD.*

PSALM 27:14

Why are you afraid? Trust God's promises!
Draw from *His* well. Take as much as you need.
Be strong! Be brave! Wait for the Lord!

# LIAR, LIAR

*The devil is a liar and the father of every lie. There is no truth in him.*

JOHN 8:44

The devil is a liar. He will try to make you think God's promises are not true. Is he trying to frighten you today? Shine the light of God's Word in his face, and he will run far away.

# HERE AND NOW

*I will see the goodness of the LORD
in the land of the living.*

PSALM 27:13

Jesus is preparing a beautiful home for you in heaven. But you don't have to wait for that day to have all the good things God promised. When you call on His name, you will see His goodness and love in your everyday life as well.

# SHOO, FLY!

*Resist the devil and he will
flee from you.*

JAMES 4:7

If you let the devil pester you, he will. How do you make him stop? Swat him with God's Word! When he whispers his ugly little lies in your ear, shout out God's promises. He will run away from God's Word every single time.

# SWING AND A MISS

*No weapon made to harm you
will prosper.*

ISAIAH 54:17

Is someone or something trying to hurt you?
Always remember this: In order for *anything* to
do you any real harm, it must get past Jesus first.

# COME AND GET IT

*You, O LORD, are a shield around me.*

PSALM 3:3

It doesn't matter who. . .it doesn't matter where. . . it doesn't matter how or why or when. . . Before *anything* can *ever* get to you, it must find a way to push God Almighty out of the way first.

# ALIVE AND POWERFUL

*The Word of God is alive and powerful,*
*sharper than a two-edged sword.*

HEBREWS 4:12

God's promises are alive and powerful. They are the weapon God gave you to defeat *everything* that tries to hurt you. Anger never makes things better. But God's truth and a heart filled with His love will disarm and defeat every foe.

# NEW EVERY MORNING

*God's love never ends. His mercy
is new every morning.*

LAMENTATIONS 3:22–23

Oops! Did you make a mess of things
yesterday? We all have from time to time. But
today is a new day. And God is ready to forgive.

# SAVED!

*God did not send His son into the world
to punish us. He sent Him to save us!*

JOHN 3:17

Sin is a prison you can never escape on your
own. That's why God sent His Son. Jesus never
sinned. He did not deserve to die. But sin must
be punished. And the punishment is death! So
Jesus took our punishment. His death on the cross
saved us from our sins. Now the prison doors are
open. Our chains are broken and we are free!

# WHITE AS SNOW

*Even though your sins
are as red as blood,
I will wash them as white as snow.*

ISAIAH 1:18

Have you sinned? Don't feel bad. Everyone has. When you ask Jesus to forgive you, the blood He shed on the cross will wash your sins away *for good*. You will be clean and pure again.

# Born Again

*"I tell you the truth,
unless you are born again,
you cannot see the kingdom of God."*

John 3:3

What does it mean to be born again?
It means sin moves out and Jesus moves in.
Jesus wants to put His love inside your heart.
But He will not force Himself on you.
He wants new life to be *your choice*. If you ask,
He will make your heart His home. The blood
Jesus shed when He died on the cross will wash
your sins away and you will be "born again."

# BLESS YOU

*Do not repay evil with evil. When you are
made fun of, don't make fun in return.
Bless others and God will bless you.*

1 PETER 3:9

People are funny. . . Some folks will try
to make you angry just for fun. Do you know
how to spoil their little game? Don't get mad.
Don't get even. Bless them instead!

# HAPPY DAYS

*Do you want to live a happy life?
Then stop using your lips to spread
bad news, rumors, and lies.*

1 PETER 3:10

**What** makes a bad day bad? Do you know?
A lot of times it's *words*. Your words can make
people feel wonderful—or they can make people
feel awful. How are you using your words today?

# I KNEW THAT

*All men will know that you are Mine
if you love one another.*

JOHN 13:35

Do people know your heart belongs to Jesus?
How? Is it the way you dress? The words you
say? Maybe. But when you truly love people
without finding fault, *they will know*. Why?
Because without God's help it cannot be done!

# WALKING IN THE LIGHT

*If we walk in the light,
as God is in the light, we will be able
to live together in peace and joy.*

1 JOHN 1:7

Are you walking in the light? Or are you stumbling along in the dark? Here's how to tell: Does your head hurt? Are your toes stubbed and sore? Is everything broken and knocked down around you? I hope not! But if those things are true, can you guess where you are?

# LIGHT OF LIFE

*I am the light of the world. Whoever
follows Me will never walk in darkness.*

JOHN 8:12

Jesus is the light of life. When you trust
His Word and follow Him, you will never
stumble along in the darkness again!

# THAT'S THE TRUTH

*You will know the truth,
and the truth will set you free.*

JOHN 8:32

Lies can only live where truth cannot be found. Have you been taken prisoner by a lie? Open up your heart. Fill it with God's Word. The truth will set you free!

# STUCK ON YOU

*There is a friend who sticks closer than a brother.*

PROVERBS 18:24

Do you have a brother, a sister, or a very best friend? Then you know how wonderful it is to be loved so very much. Friends will come and go. That's just a part of life. But Jesus will *never* leave you or take away His love.

# THE GOOD SHEPHERD

*I am the Good Shepherd. . .
I lay my life down for the sheep.*

JOHN 10:14–15

Sheep are funny little creatures. They love to wander off and get into trouble. You and I are like that, aren't we? We both need a *shepherd*. Jesus is our shepherd. He loves us so much He gave up *His* life so we could be safe in God's arms forever.

# BECAUSE I WANTED TO

*No one took My life from Me.*
*I gave it up because I wanted to.*

JOHN 10:18

Why didn't Jesus save Himself when He was on the cross? That's a good question. The answer is simple: *He wanted to save you.*

# THE DOOR

*I am the door.*
*All who come through Me will be saved.*

JOHN 10:9

There is only one door that opens into heaven. But it's not hard to find. *Jesus* is the door. And God promises that *everyone* who walks through that door will be saved.

# KNOCK

*Knock, and the door will open.*

MATTHEW 7:7

The door to heaven is not locked. Would you like to come in? All you have to do is knock. Jesus is waiting to open the door and pour every blessing of heaven into your heart today.

# ASK

*Ask, and it will be given to you.*

MATTHEW 7:7

Do you want Jesus to come into your heart? All you have to do is ask. Here's how to start: *Jesus, here is my heart. Please make my heart Your home. I'm sorry for the things I've done wrong and I want to change. Please take my life and make it everything You ever wanted it to be.*

# YOU FOUND ME

*Seek and you will find.*

MATTHEW 7:7

Jesus is not hiding. When you look for Him, *you will find Him.* And when you find Him, you will find everything you will ever need.

# TEARS OF JOY

*I will turn your sorrow into gladness.*

JEREMIAH 31:13

Sometimes tears are the only song
a broken and lonely heart can sing. But tears
can bring healing as well. Jesus knows your
heart. He knows how you feel. *If you let Him,*
He will wipe away your tears with love.

# WHAT DID I SAY?

*A man's wisdom teaches him how
to wait, hold his tongue, and forgive.*

PROVERBS 19:11

Did you ever say something you wish you could take back? There's just no way to stuff those words back in your mouth, is there? Nope! But mistakes can become lessons—*and even blessings*—if you learn from them and try to do what God says next time.

# STRONG TOWER

*The name of the Lord is a strong tower.*
*The godly run to Him and are safe.*

PROVERBS 18:10

Why do you build a fort? To keep your enemy out, of course! But a fort is only as strong as the stuff it's made of. Is someone trying to hurt you or make you do something wrong? Run to Jesus. No one can huff and puff and blow *that* house down!

# You've Got Mail

*You are a love letter from Jesus,*
*written not with ink, but with*
*the Spirit of the living God.*

2 Corinthians 3:3

Your life is a love letter to the people all
around you. Open it up and let everyone
read about the amazing things Jesus can do!

# FROM YOUR HEART

*God gave us all the skill we need
to share His love with others.*

2 CORINTHIANS 3:6

Do you ever feel like you want to tell someone about God's love, but just don't know what to say? Don't worry. You won't make a mistake. Speak from your heart and watch what God will do!

# FAITHFUL

*He who began a good work in you
will be faithful to complete it.*

PHILIPPIANS 1:6

Jesus put a special dream deep inside your
heart. You know what it is. You know what to do.
*Trust Him.* He will make that dream come true!

# BOLD AND STRONG

*Be strong. Be brave. Don't be afraid.*
*I will be with you wherever you go.*

JOSHUA 1:9

Where are you going today? What are you going to do? Whatever it is, you don't need to worry. Jesus is already waiting there for you!

# OF COURSE NOT

*Is anything too hard for the LORD?*

GENESIS 18:14

Jesus loves you. He hears you when you pray. He made the heavens, the earth, and *everything* in them. There is nothing too big or too small, too hard, *or too easy* for Him!

# BEAUTIFUL

*Give thanks to the LORD for He is good.*
*His love will be yours forever.*

PSALM 118:1

It's a beautiful day today, isn't it? God's love is flowing in and out of everything like a cool breath of fresh, clean air. So take a minute and thank Him. Tell Him how much you love Him. God is good and His love will be yours *forever!*

# I CAN SEE CLEARLY

*We have the mind of Christ.*

1 CORINTHIANS 2:16

Jesus wants to teach you many new things. Some of those things are easy to learn. Others can take a very long time to get right. But *His heart* is in *your* heart. And IIis mind is in your mind. The help you need is only a prayer away.

# YOU CAN KNOW

*God gave us His Spirit
so we can know about all the
wonderful things He has done for us.*

1 CORINTHIANS 2:12

When a man does not have Jesus in his heart he cannot admit that God's Word is true. Without God's heart and mind, it doesn't make sense. It all seems foolish—and he cannot understand why God would give us all these wonderful things for free.

# WILL YOU CARRY ME?

*The one the LORD loves
will rest between his shoulders.*

DEUTERONOMY 33:12

Have you ever been so tired from walking that you needed your daddy to pick you up and carry you on his shoulders? It's fun to be up so high, isn't it? Are you sad or lonely today? Let Jesus carry you. You're small and light. Your Daddy loves you, and He is happy to do it.

# COOL IT!

*A hot-tempered man stirs up anger and
bad feelings, but a patient man calms
them before they turn into a fight.*

PROVERBS 15:18

Anger is like soup made from everyone's
garbage. It's ready to boil over at the slightest
touch. Don't be the one who stirs the pot!

# PAY BACK

*Dear friends, don't try to get even. Let God take care of that. "I will punish those who do wrong," says the Lord.*

ROMANS 12:19

Did someone say or do something mean to you? You'd like to get them back, wouldn't you? Anger *always* makes things worse. Next time pray, *forgive,* and let God take care of the rest.

# I Give Up

*The LORD gives strength to the weary and power to the weak.*

ISAIAH 40:29

When someone is ready to give up, what do they need? Your kindness, courage, and support will bring back hope. That will blow dark clouds away and begin to make everything better again.

# A Helping Hand

*When you offer each other a helping hand, you obey the law of Christ.*

GALATIANS 6:2

We all need a little help now and then. There's nothing wrong with that. Do you need some help? Don't be afraid to ask. Does someone need *your* help? *Show them what God's love can do!*

# PEACE

*I will give you peace in the land.*
*You will lie down and no one*
*will make you afraid.*

LEVITICUS 26:6

Without Jesus, you will never have peace.
But when Jesus lives in your heart, you will be
able to find peace no matter how crazy your
life becomes.

# BLESSED

*Blessed is the man
who trusts in the LORD.*

PSALM 40:4

What does it mean to be blessed? It means God loves you more than anything in the whole world—and *every* good thing He has is yours!

# POOR IN SPIRIT

*Blessed are the poor in spirit, for the kingdom of heaven belongs to them.*

MATTHEW 5:3

Have you reached the end of your rope? Do you know deep down in your heart that without Jesus you won't make it even one more day? *Then you are blessed*—and all of heaven belongs to you!

# THOSE WHO MOURN

*Blessed are those who mourn,*
*for they will be comforted.*

## MATTHEW 5:4

Do you feel the terrible pain that comes when you've lost someone you love very much? Then run into the arm of the One who loves you most.

# MEEK

*Blessed are the meek,*
*for they will inherit the earth.*

## MATTHEW 5:5

Would you like to inherit the earth? It's easy! Just be gentle, quiet, polite, kind, and don't get upset when people try to take your stuff. One day, the whole thing will fall right into your lap.

# HUNGER AND THIRST

*Blessed are those who hunger and thirst
to be like God, for they will be filled.*

MATTHEW 5:6

Do you know someone who loves to eat?
I do, too! When your heart is hungry and
thirsty to become more like Jesus, He will
make every day a Thanksgiving feast.

# MERCY

*Blessed are the merciful,*
*for they will be shown mercy.*

MATTHEW 5:7

Kindness is a little thing, but it makes
a big difference to everyone who receives it.
Is your heart filled with this special gift?
Pour its gentle beauty into everyone you meet.

# PURE IN HEART

*Blessed are the pure in heart,*
*for they will see God.*

MATTHEW 5:8

What does Jesus look like? Do you know? When your heart belongs to Him, you will get to find out. One day you will step out of this world *forever*. You will step into heaven where you will see Jesus face-to-face!

# PEACEMAKERS

*Blessed are the peacemakers,*
*for they will be called the sons of God.*

MATTHEW 5:9

Do you know that you are a teacher? That's right! Your life will either show people how to forgive and live together, or it will show them how to fight and destroy everything they love.

# A Great Reward

*When people hurt you, lie about you, and call you names because you love Me, your reward in heaven is great.*

MATTHEW 5:11–12

Loving Jesus will not make everyone love *you*. It will make some people very angry. Don't let that bother you. Keep on loving them. God will do something amazing for them *and for you!*

# That's What He Said

*I am the LORD.*
*I do not change.*

MALACHI 3:6

When God says something, you can believe it! His promises are real. They are yours *forever*. He won't ever change His mind or take His promises away.

# I'll Say it Again

*Jesus Christ is the same yesterday, today, and forever.*

Hebrews 13:8

Do you know someone who is happy one day and grumpy the next? God's love is never, *ever* like that. He loved you yesterday. He loves you today. And He will love you forever and ever.

# CARRIED AWAY

*He took our sickness upon Himself
and carried it away.*

MATTHEW 8:17

Have you ever read Matthew chapter eight? When sick people asked Jesus to make them well, what did Jesus do? *He made them well!* He will do the same for you today. Do you believe it?

# WE ARE HEALED

*By His wounds we are healed.*

ISAIAH 53:5

**Why** was Jesus punished? *It was because we have sinned.* It's true! He was bruised for all the terrible things we did wrong. He took our sickness. He carried our sorrow. His punishment gave us peace, and by His wounds *we are healed!*

# ALL WHO TOUCHED HIM

*All who touched Him were healed.*

MATTHEW 14:36

When sick people came to Jesus and asked to be made well, how many did He make well? That's right—*all of them*. God's Word says, "All who touched Him were healed!"

# HE KNOWS

*Not a single sparrow can fall to the ground without your Father knowing it.*

MATTHEW 10:29

Jesus knows everything about you. If your heart is broken, His is too. You don't have to worry. He will take care of everything. You can never remember *anything* that God will forget.

# Yes, You!

*I will pour out My Spirit
on all the people.*

Acts 2:17

God's gifts are for *everyone*. You are never too young. You are never too old. When your heart belongs to Jesus, God will open up heaven and pour every good thing into *your* life as well.

# LIFE AND PEACE

*A heart that follows after God's Spirit*
*is filled with life and peace.*

ROMANS 8:6

When you want everything you can get your hands on, you will be stuck with a lot of stuff you wish you never had! But when you want what *God* wants, *when* God wants you to have it, your heart and your mind will be filled with peace and joy.

# EVEN HIS ENEMIES

*When a man's ways please the LORD,
even his enemies will be
at peace with him.*

PROVERBS 16:7

Has someone been very mean to you again?
Do you want him to stop? Take God's advice!
Did he steal your hat? *Don't get mad.* Hunt him
down and give him your coat!

# PERFECT PEACE

*The LORD will give perfect peace
to every heart that trusts in Him.*

ISAIAH 26:3

Do you know someone whose heart and
mind are filled with worry, panic, fear, and
doubt? Share your heart with them today
and watch what God's amazing love can do!

# SONGS OF JOY

*Those who sow in tears
will reap with songs of joy.*

PSALM 126:5

Is your heart heavy because your friend
is hurting? Keep on praying. Let your tears
water the seeds of faith God's love has planted.
Soon God will answer and you will dance
together with songs of thanks and joy.

# I'VE GOT YOU

*Give your worries to the LORD.*
*He will take care of you.*
*He will not let you slip or fall.*

PSALM 55:22

Don't worry. Everyone falls down now and then. Jesus loves you more than *anything*. He's holding your hand right now and He won't ever let go—no matter what.

# HONESTLY!

*If God is for us,
who can be against us?*

ROMANS 8:31

God is not mad at you. *He loves you!*
He is absolutely, completely, 100 percent
on your side. *Everything* He has is yours.
Nothing can ever take away His love.

# MAYBE TODAY

*I am coming soon!*

REVELATION 22:7

Jesus is coming back soon! It may be today. It may be tomorrow. Only God knows for sure. *But He is coming.* That is a promise. Are you ready to see Him? Oh, what a day that will be!

# ONE WAY

*I am the way, the truth, and the life.*
*No one can come to the Father*
*except through Me.*

JOHN 14:6

How do you get to heaven? People have a lot of different answers for that question. But God says there is only one road that will take you there. And there is only one door that will let you come in. That road and that door *is Jesus!*

# AMAZING!

*I tell you the truth,*
*whoever believes in Me*
*will do the same things that I do.*

JOHN 14:12

Jesus did some amazing things, didn't He?
Now He says if you believe in Him, *you* can
those same amazing things as well!

# EVEN GREATER

*Those who believe will do
even greater things than these,
because I am going to the Father.*

JOHN 14:12

Jesus said you can do the same things He did.
But He didn't stop there. He also said those who
believe will do *even greater things* than He did!
So tell me. . . *Do you believe it?*

# I WILL DO IT

*If you ask for anything
in My name, I will do it.*

JOHN 14:14

Jesus is happy when we ask Him for help. It proves we trust Him and believe what He says. So don't be afraid. Ask Him right now! What's the *best* thing that could happen?

# WORTHLESS IDOLS

*Those who cling to worthless idols give up the grace that could be theirs.*

JONAH 2:8

What is an idol? It's someone or something you love and adore that doesn't love and adore you in return. It's like a broken promise. When you trust an idol, you will end up broken as well.

# THE HOLY PLACE

*The man who will not give his heart to an idol may come into God's Holy Place and receive His blessing.*

PSALM 24:3–5

Why does God want you to love Him more than you love anything or anyone else? Because He knows that people and things, *no matter how good they are,* will one day break your heart.

# CLEAN HANDS

*Who may come into God's Holy Place?*
*Anyone who has clean hands*
*and a pure heart.*

PSALM 24:3–4

Where have you been? What have you been
doing? Have you done something wrong? Don't
worry. Jesus loves you. He wants to make you
clean again. Give Him your hands. *Give Him*
*your heart.* Come as you are. He will forgive!

# FOREVER

*The Word of our God will stand forever.*

ISAIAH 40:8

Summertime! Don't you wish it would last forever? I do, too. But before you know it, the flowers will be gone and the grass will be covered with snow. Oh, bother! But that's okay. There's really only one thing that never changes. And nothing can ever take that away!

# SING YOUR PRAISE

*Oh, how You bless those*
*who live in Your house!*
*They will sing Your praise forever.*

PSALM 84:4

Jesus loves to hear your heart singing beautiful songs of thanksgiving and praise. So don't hold back. Open up your heart. Let His love pour in. Tell Him how you feel. *Sing praise to the Lord!*

# A PLACE OF JOY!

*When you walk through
the Valley of Weeping
it will become a place of joy.*

PSALM 84:5–6

Your happy heart and the strength that comes from knowing Jesus are just what your friend needs. Don't be afraid of her sadness and tears. Step into her darkness and shine God's light!

# My Pleasure

*God will gladly give you
the wisdom you need.
All you have to do is ask.*

JAMES 1:5

Some folks can get a little crabby when you ask them for help. Is God like that? Not at all. Jesus loves you. He won't ever get upset when you ask Him to show you the right thing to do.

# THE RIGHT CHOICE

*Wisdom will save you
from the ways of evil men.*

PROVERBS 2:12

It's not always easy to make the right choice.
People say so many things. And *everyone* thinks
they are right. But when you have the courage
to say, "no" you are shining God's light, whether
others choose to see that light or not.

# As Iron Sharpens Iron

*Just like iron sharpens iron,
one friend sharpens another.*

Proverbs 27:17

Do you have a friend who loves Jesus with all his heart? A friend like that is a special gift. When you are that kind of friend to someone else, you are exactly where God wants you to be!

# By Faith

*God's children will live by faith!*

Romans 1:17

Jesus loves you. Everything you need is just a prayer away. So trust Him today. Trust Him with your life. Trust Him with your heart. He is God *Almighty*. You are safe in His loving arms.

# I Can Do All Things

*I can do all things through*
*Christ who gives me strength.*

Philippians 4:13

"All things" means *all things*, or it doesn't mean anything. Is there a mountain standing in your way? Don't ever shrink back and say, "It can't be done." *You know it can*—if you look to Jesus!

# Everything

*The Lord is my shepherd.*
*I will always have everything I need.*

Psalm 23:1

Jesus is your shepherd. And you are His precious little lamb. When you trust Him and put your life in His hands, He promises you will always have everything you need.

# STILL WATERS

*The LORD is my shepherd. . .*
*He leads me beside still waters.*

PSALM 23:2

Has someone been stirring your pot? Have they been tossing and spinning you around and around? Has your peace all sloshed out? Jesus has a quiet place where you can get away and rest. Why not let Him take you there today?

# HUFF AND PUFF...

*The LORD is my shepherd. . .*
*I will not be afraid.*

PSALM 23:4

Every now and then people and things will come along and try to huff and puff and blow your house down. Don't let that bother you. Jesus knows all about it. Trust Him. Let Him take care of it. He is working for your good.

# COVERED

*The LORD will cover you with his feathers.*
*He will shelter you under his wings.*

PSALM 91:4

Have you ever had one of those days where nothing seems to go right? Yes, it's no fun. But that's no reason to stand out in the cold. God's arms are open wide. His heart is safe and warm. Come inside. Let Him cover you with love today.

# A Strong Tower

*If you make the LORD your refuge,*
*no evil will be able to overpower you.*

PSALM 91:9–10

A refuge is a place you run to for safety. Is something or someone trying to hurt you? Run into God's arms as fast as you can. Trust His promises. Believe what He says! God can do miracles—*and He will do them for you.*

# GREATER IS HE

*God's Spirit is alive in you and He is greater than the spirit of all God's enemies who live in this world.*

1 JOHN 4:4

Think about it! God Almighty, who made the earth, the sky, and *everything* in them, is alive in your heart right now. Who could ever hope to fight against Him or take His love away?

# HIS!

*The Lord knows those who are His.*

2 TIMOTHY 2:19

**Jesus** knows you by name. He loves you just the way you are. You don't ever have to worry. He won't forget you. He will always be with you. You will always have everything you need.

# NEW LIFE

*Everyone who belongs to Jesus
will be given new life.*

1 CORINTHIANS 15:22

New life is not just a feeling like the goose-
bumps or a friendly tickle. New life is the gift
that Jesus gives to all who give their heart
completely to Him.

# JUST AS I PLANNED

*I know the plans I have for you. They are
plans to prosper you, not to harm you;
plans to give you a future and hope.*

JEREMIAH 29:11

Jesus has a wonderful plan for your life.
He is not mad at you. He wants to help you.
And Jesus promises that *He will help you*
when you trust Him with all your heart.

# TOGETHER FOR GOOD

*All things work together for the good of those who love God, for they belong to Him, just as He always wanted.*

ROMANS 8:28

God is always working for your good. No matter what happens—*good or bad*—He will pick up the pieces of your life and put them back together to make something beautiful.

# PEACE AND STRENGTH

*The LORD gives strength to His children
and blesses them with peace.*

PSALM 29:11

**Where** does true strength come from? Does it come from winning all the time? Does it come from always being right? Not really. Peace and strength are twins—two beautiful gifts given to a heart that longs to be filled with God's love.

# YOU ARE MY KING

*If you honestly say, "Jesus is Lord,"*
*and believe in your heart God raised*
*Him from the dead, you will be saved.*

ROMANS 10:9

Who sits on the throne of your life? A throne is for a king. The one who sits there is born to rule. When you are ready to step down from that seat and bow before the One True King, God will give you new life—and you will be born again.

# A GIFT FROM GOD

*You have been saved by grace because of your faith. You can't take any credit for it. It is a gift from God.*

EPHESIANS 2:8

New life is a gift. *God gives it for free.* You can't earn it by doing good or being good. No matter how hard you try, it will never be enough. Why? Because Jesus already paid the price. God gives new life when you open up *your heart.*

# NOT A REWARD

*New life is a gift, not a reward for the good things we have done, so none of us can boast that we did it ourselves.*

EPHESIANS 2:8–9

New life is not a reward you get for doing good or being good or going to church. Those things are good. But they will not get you into heaven. *New life is a gift.* Why would you try to pay for it if God will give it to you for free?

# I Did it My Way

*Everyone who hears My words
and does not do them is like a foolish
man who built his house on sand.*

Matthew 7:26

When you hear what God says but choose
to do things your own way, you are like a man
building his house on the sand. Everything is
fine now. But soon the waves will come—and
in the blink of an eye it will all be washed away.

# GOOD AND PERFECT

*The LORD will never withhold
any good thing from those
who do what pleases Him.*

PSALM 84:11

Jesus loves you. When you live in a way that
is pleasing to Him, God will gladly move heaven
and earth to make sure you have every good and
perfect gift you need.

# I Can Only Imagine

*No eye has seen, no ear has heard,
no mind can imagine what God has
in store for those who love Him.*

1 CORINTHIANS 2:9

Do you like to open presents? What was the best gift you ever received? Jesus wants to give you a gift so incredible that when you finally see it, you won't believe your eyes.

# HE DOES NOT LIE

*God is not a man. He does not lie
or change His mind.*

NUMBERS 23:19

God's promises are so amazing that many good people have a hard time believing they are true. Don't let that bother you. God does not lie. His promises are yours *forever*. Nothing can make Him change His mind or take away His love.

# WE CAN SURELY DO IT

*Let us go up and take the land*
*for we can surely do it.*

NUMBERS 13:30

**What** do you want to do when you grow up? Who do you want to be? Your dreams are not stupid or silly. They were planted in your heart by God. And when *your* dreams are *God's* dreams, *your dreams will come true.*

# STEP ON IT!

*Wherever your feet go,
I will give you the land.*

JOSHUA 1:3

Take a look at your feet. Are they going where Jesus wants them to go? Are they doing the things Jesus wants them to do? If so, every place you set your foot will be yours *to change for the better* with the good news of God's love.

# I Tell You the Truth

*If you have faith as small as a mustard seed you can tell this mountain to move and it will move. Nothing will be impossible for you.*

Matthew 17:20

Is there a mountain in your life that is too tall to go over or too big to go around? Jesus said, "Tell it to move." Remember, God is not a man. He does not lie. So trust His promises. Wait for Him to act, and then watch what He will do!

# IT'S THAT SIMPLE

*Anyone who will not accept
the Kingdom of God like a little child
will never enter it.*

MARK 10:15

Why is it so hard for some people to trust Jesus and believe the things He says? Why would anyone turn and walk away when Jesus loves them so much and wants to give them so many good things? I just don't know.

# OUCH!

*Watch out! If you keep on biting and clawing each other, be careful or you will tear each other apart.*

GALATIANS 5:15

Anger and cruel words never make anything better. When you see that *you* are the one to blame, make sure you stop at once.

# PLEASE FORGIVE ME

*Whoever admits his sin
and turns away from it
will be forgiven.*

PROVERBS 28:13

Did you hurt someone very much? There's no reason to cover it up. There's no reason to pretend it never happened. Tell him you're sorry. Then tell Jesus, too. He will wash your sin away.

# GOOD WORK

*A good man gives freely to the poor
and will be greatly praised.*

PSALM 112:9

Do you knows someone who needs help?
Jesus has a special gift in store *for you* when
you help others when and where you can.

# FIRST AND BEST

*Give God the first and best
of all you own and you will have
more than you will ever need.*

PROVERBS 3:9–10

Do you have a lot of stuff, or just a little?
Do you love to share your good things with God
and with others? When you give God *your very
best*, God will give *His* very best to you.

# TOMORROW

*If you can help your neighbor today, help him today. Don't ask him to come back tomorrow.*

PROVERBS 3:28

Do you have more than enough of something your friend needs very badly? If you can help him today, don't make him wait until tomorrow.

# No Thanks

*Give freely to those in need without judgment or ill-will, and God will bless your work and the things you do.*

DEUTERONOMY 15:10

There will be days when you give and give and give with no thanks. Sometimes you'll never get *anything* in return. Remember, God sees the good you do. When your heart is right, *He* will reward you even when others do not.

# CHEER UP!

*God loves a cheerful giver.*

2 CORINTHIANS 9:7

Are you a happy, cheery, jolly, smiling, joyful, merry giver *and liver?* Your friends will always be glad that you are such a special part of their day—and Jesus will be, too!

# SQUEEZED

*Be brave. Be strong. Do not be afraid.
The LORD is with you. He will never leave
you or take away His love.*

DEUTERONOMY 31:6

Are your knobby knees knocking? Is your little heart pounding? Are you ready to run away and hide? *Hold your ground!* Trust the Lord. To get the juice, the fruit must be squeezed!

# My Pleasure

*Fear not, little flock.*
*It is your Father's great pleasure*
*to give you the kingdom.*

Luke 12:32

What do you need right now? *Whatever it is,* Jesus already has it. So don't worry about it for one more minute. Tell Him what you need. He is ready and waiting to help you today.

# FAITH PLEASE!

*Without faith
it is impossible to please God.*

HEBREWS 11:6

Do you know how to make God happy?
Trust Him! Fill your heart with His promises.
Put your life in His hands. *Give Him all the
pieces* and let Him make something beautiful.

# I BELIEVE IT

*He who comes to God must believe that God is real and that He rewards those who seek Him with all their heart.*

HEBREWS 11:6

God is real. You did not think Him up inside your head. *He thought you up inside His!* Are you hiding His promises deep down in your heart? Good! God has good things in store when you trust Him and put your life in His hands.

# BREAD ON THE WATER

*Cast your bread on the water,
and after many days
you will find it again.*

ECCLESIASTES 11:1

This is a very unusual promise, isn't it?
Do you know what it means? God says when
you do good things for others, those good
things find their way back to you when *you*
are in need!

# TEST ME AND SEE!

*Test me and see! I will open the gates of heaven and pour out so much blessing you won't have room to hold it.*

MALACHI 3:10

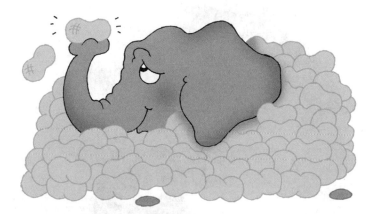

Can a man rob God? And even if he could, why would he be foolish enough to try? When you give back the first and best part of everything God gives you, He will bury you under so much blessing, you won't be able to take it all in.

# I Am Free

*Because you belong to Jesus,
the power of His Spirit has freed you
from the power of sin and death.*

ROMANS 8:2

God's Spirit brings life wherever He goes.
When I truly allow God's Holy Spirit to show
me how to live, sin has no power to make me
do anything that would break God's heart.

# WE ARE HIS CHILDREN

*God's Spirit speaks to our hearts
and tells us we are His children.*

## ROMANS 8:16

Do you know how to listen to your heart?
Not just the *thump-thump* part, but the part
God is filling with His goodness and love?
That's where Jesus lives. God's heart—*alive in
our hearts*—is the proof that we are His children.

# HELP YOURSELF

*Since we are God's children,
everything He has is ours as well.*

ROMANS 8:17

You are God's beloved child. *Everything* He
has is yours. What do you need today? Courage?
Patience? Wisdom? *A miracle?* Jesus has more
than enough. And all of it belongs to you.

# WHY, OH WHY?

*But if we are to share God's glory,
we must also share His suffering.*

ROMANS 8:17

No one likes to suffer. That's no surprise. But there are times you may have to suffer for *doing the right thing*. That doesn't seem fair. But remember, Jesus sees what we cannot. And He *always* works everything out for the good of those who love Him.

# Simple Enough!

*Treat other people the way
you want them to treat you.*

MATTHEW 7:12

Have you ever tried to love someone who
is always mean and unkind? It's not easy, is it?
Many things Jesus says seem pretty simple at
first—until you try to do them yourself!

# LIGHT OF THE WORLD

*You are the light
of the world.*

MATTHEW 5:14

Who is the light of the world? You are! So shine your light. Let the things you say and do show everyone around you God's love is real.

# City on a Hill

*A city on a hill
cannot be hidden.*

MATTHEW 5:14

When you light a lamp, what do you do with it? Do you put it in a box? Do you hide it under the bed? Of course not. You set it on a stand so everyone can see the light!

# WHEREVER YOU GO

*I will watch over you wherever you go and do all I have promised.*

GENESIS 28:15

Jesus loves you more than *anything* in the world. He will never leave you. He will never take His love away. Wherever you go, whatever you do, you will always be safe in His loving arms.

# THAT'S THE TRUTH

*Truthful words will last forever,*
*but lies are quickly uncovered.*

PROVERBS 12:19

Lies are like weeds. They spread out quickly and hide the truth beneath a tangled, ugly mess that's easy to spot. And—like weeds—they tangle, trip, snare, cut, rip, and leave behind prickles, burs, and stings that are very hard to get out.

# AN HONEST MAN

*An honest man tells the truth,
but a dishonest man lies and lies.*

PROVERBS 14:5

Have you ever been to the dentist? Did he give you a shot to make your mouth numb? Lies are a lot like that shot. The more you lie, the less you can feel —or see—the terrible pain your lies bring to yourself and to everyone around you.

# HONESTLY!

*A person who does what is right
and speaks the truth will be safe, sound,
and have the good things he needs.*

ISAIAH 33:15–16

God loves the truth. And why wouldn't He?
*He is the Truth!* And He promises to reward
you for being honest in all the big and little
things that come your way today.

# PEACE IS A GIFT

*Don't worry about anything; pray about everything! Tell God what you need. Thank Him for all He's done and God's peace will guard your heart and mind as you trust Him.*

PHILIPPIANS 4:6–7

Peace is a gift that comes from God. It can't be bought at any price. That's why so few people have it. But when you trust God, pray, and *refuse to worry*, He will give peace for free. How? No one really knows. But He will. Try it—you'll see!

# PEACE IN MY HEART

*The peace I have, I give to you.
My peace is a gift the world
does not have and cannot give.*

JOHN 14:27

Peace is a gift our world wants but does not seem to have. Why? Because Jesus is the gift our world needs—but does not seem to want!

# And Proud of It

*The Lord opposes the proud but gives grace to the humble.*

Proverbs 3:34

Do you know someone who thinks they know better than everyone else? Do they seem happy— *ever?* Of course not! Do you know why? When a person tells God they don't need His help, God takes His help away—and they are left to face the world and everything in it on their own.

# MORE THAN ANYTHING

*Seek the LORD and you will live.*

AMOS 5:6

What are you looking for? What do you want more than *anything else* in the whole, wide world? When the treasure your heart longs to hold is Jesus, you will find it—and you will live!

# LIVING BREAD

*I am the living bread that came down from heaven. If you eat this bread, you will live forever.*

JOHN 6:51

Jesus said, "I am the bread of life." When you eat *this* bread—when you give your heart to Jesus, learn to walk in His ways, fill your mind with His promises, trust Him, and pray—you will live and be happy both now and *forever!*

# Living Water

*Is anyone thirsty? Come to me and drink. When you believe in me, streams of living water will flow from your heart.*

John 7:37–38

Remember, the gifts Jesus gives are for you *and everyone around you*. Don't forget to share God's goodness and love with someone who needs them today!

# BROKENHEARTED

*The LORD heals the brokenhearted
and binds up their wounds.*

PSALM 147:3

Have you ever had a broken heart? Some days it feels like the pain will never get better. Jesus knows how you feel. He has the healing you need. Let Him bind up the wound that has hurt you so much. He wants to set you free.

# FROM THEM ALL

*A godly man faces many troubles,
but the LORD delivers him from them all.*

PSALM 34:19

Are you having "one of those days" again?
Don't let that steal your joy. *God is not mad at you.*
He loves you! Trouble may come. But God's help
is already on the way. So give Him thanks and
hold your ground. He will be there right on time.

# First Things First

*Seek God's kingdom first and He will
give you everything you need.*

Luke 21:31

Can I ask you a couple of silly questions? Okay,
here goes: Do birds worry about running out of
worms? Do flowers get upset because they aren't
pretty enough? Then why work and worry over
things God *will give you for free* when all you really
need to do is open up your heart and let Him in?

# START LIVING YOURS

*The Good Shepherd
lays down His life for the sheep.*

JOHN 10:11

Do you ever wonder if Jesus really loves you?
I know at times it can be hard to believe.
But think about this: Jesus was willing to stop
living His life so you could start living yours.
If that isn't love, what in the world is?

# PERFECT LOVE

*Perfect love drives out fear.*

1 JOHN 4:18

God is not mad at you. He knows about the good things you do. He knows about the bad things, too. You can't hide the bad things. Those things must change. But God loves you. He will help you. Let Him come and change your heart.

# I Am the Vine

*I am the vine. You are the branches.*
*If you are cut off from me*
*you can do nothing.*

John 15:5

When you pick a flower, what happens
to it after awhile? It shrivels up and dies! Why?
Because it's been cut off from its source of life.
Jesus is your source of life. Don't ever let *anything*
come along and pluck you away from His love.

# YOU ARE THE BRANCHES

*I am the vine. You are the branches.*
*When you live in Me, and I live in you,*
*you will bear much fruit.*

JOHN 15:5

But when a flower is *not* cut off, what happens? That's right—it blooms and grows and makes seeds that will soon give birth to hundreds of other beautiful flowers for everyone to enjoy.

# POWER FOREVER

*My saving power will last forever.*

ISAIAH 51:8

**Batteries** go dead. Light bulbs burn out. Cars run out of gas. Friends get sleepy and need to take a nap. But God's amazing power to love and to save will go on and on *forever!*

# TIME TO WAKE UP

*A little more sleep, a little more slumber,
a little more folding the hands to rest—
and suddenly all you have is gone!*

PROVERBS 6:10–11

A little bit of sleep is good. A lot of sleep
is *wonderful*. But too much sleep is a thief.
It will rob you of everything your faith in
God and hard work have made possible.

# My Girl

*Charm can fool you. And beauty will fade away. But a woman who loves the Lord will be praised.*

Proverbs 31:30

Do you know someone special who is very beautiful *on the inside?* That kind of beauty— the beauty Jesus gives—is a blessing to everyone, a trap to no one. It will never, ever fade away.

# THAT'S GOOD!

*The LORD is good.*

NAHUM 1:7

What is God like? There are many ways to answer that question. When you look at the answers what do you find? That's right—they all say the very same thing—*God is good!*

# THAT'S BETTER!

*The LORD is good. He is a shelter in times of trouble*

NAHUM 1:7

Trouble will come. That doesn't mean God is mad at you. It doesn't mean He took His love away. Trust Him! Run into God's arms. He will keep you safe and wash your fear away.

# 'THAT'S A PROMISE

*The LORD is good. . .*
*He cares for those who trust in Him.*

NAHUM 1:7

Jesus promises to take care of *everyone* who trusts Him. Do you trust Him today? Good! When you trust God's Word and believe what He says, trouble may come—*but it cannot stay!*

# HERE TO STAY

*Stay in Me,*
*and I will stay in you.*

JOHN 15:4

Jesus made your heart His home. Now He wants *you* to make *His heart* your home. When you stay close to Jesus in every way, God's love will flow in, out, and through all you say and do.

# ANYTHING

*If you live in Me and my words
live in you, you may ask for anything
you want and it will be done for you.*

JOHN 15:7

This is quite a promise, isn't it? Think about it! Does Jesus live in your heart? Do you live in a way that is pleasing to Him? Jesus says when you want what God wants, you can ask Him for anything—*anything*—and He will do it!

# CONFIDENCE

*Do not throw away your confident trust in the Lord. It will be richly rewarded.*

HEBREWS 10:35

Remember, without faith it's impossible to please God. When you ask for His help, you must believe that He lives—and that He will reward you when you seek Him with all your heart.

# IN HIS HANDS

*The king's heart
is in the hand of the Lord.*

PROVERBS 21:1

Your life is in good hands! And those same hands hold the hearts and minds of everyone around you. Is someone or something causing you to worry and fret? Tell God about it. Trust Him to act and watch what He will do!

# FOOTPRINTS

*I will give you every place
you set your foot.*

JOSHUA 1:3

**Where** do you want to go today? What do
you want to do? Jesus is already waiting for you
there! When your heart and your hands belong
to Him, He will make your dreams come true.

# HE KEEPS HIS PROMISES

*The LORD your God is God!*
*He keeps His promise of love*
*to a thousand generations.*

DEUTERONOMY 7:9

God's promises are yours forever. No one can ever change them or take a single one away!

# Not Easily Broken

*A cord of three strands
is not easily broken.*

Ecclesiastes 4:12

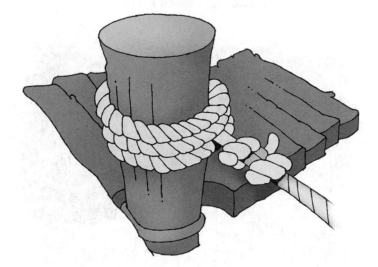

One person standing alone can be attacked and defeated. Two people standing together can fight and win. But a rope made of three parts and wound tightly together is not easily broken.

# LIKE THE SON

*Put your plans in God's hands, trust Him, and He will make your honesty and good intentions shine like the sun.*

PSALM 37:5–6

People won't always like you for doing things God's way. They may even become angry. But don't let that stop you. One day they will see that you were right, and their hearts may be changed, all because of you.

# SILENCE!

*Every tongue that tries
to accuse you will be silenced.*

ISAIAH 54:17

Is someone very angry at you for doing the right thing? Don't be afraid. Speak the truth without fear. God's Word is light. It will chase the darkness away and it will never be seen again.

# TURN, TURN, TURN

*There is a season for everything,*
*and a proper time for every purpose*
*and plan in heaven and on the earth.*

ECCLESIASTES 3:1

Can a farmer pick an apple before he plants a tree? Of course not! God knows just the right time to make your dream come true. Don't get in a hurry. Give Him time. Let your dreams grow in the way, place, and time God desires.

# Amazing Love

*There is not enough water
in the whole, wide world
to put out the fire of God's love.*

SONG OF SOLOMON 8:7

God's love is like a fire that can not be slowed down or put out by *anything*. Nothing can make it stop. And there's nowhere to hide. His love will find you—you can be sure of that. And when it does, you will never, *ever* be the same again!

# COME ON IN!

*Let us come boldly before the throne of our loving God, for we will find kindness and help when we need it the most.*

HEBREWS 4:16

Jesus loves you. You don't *ever* have to be afraid to ask Him for the things you need. You're not bothering Him. *He wants to help you.* Tell Him what you need. Let Him touch your heart today.

# MORE THAN CONQUERORS

*In all these things we are
more than conquerors because
of God who loves us.*

ROMANS 8:37

What can separate you from the love of God?
Trouble? Hardship? Hunger? Sickness? Death?
No! Jesus defeated every enemy you will ever face.
Nothing can separate you from the love of God!

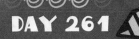

# By Faith

*Everyone whose heart
belongs to Jesus will live by faith.*

GALATIANS 3:11

It's good to be good. Are you good? Good!
But you can be "good" without God! That's
why Jesus doesn't want you just to be "good."
He wants you to *trust Him* and live your life in
a way that shouts, *"Every word God says is true!"*

# RIGHT AND GOOD

*No one's heart is made right with God by doing right or being good.*

## GALATIANS 3:11

There's nothing wrong with doing right. And there's nothing bad about being good! But no amount of doing right or being good will ever take your sin away. Only Jesus can do that.

# CALL HIM UP!

*Everyone who calls on the name of the Lord will be saved.*

ACTS 2:21

What can wash away your sin? Nothing but the blood of Jesus! How do you get washed by His blood? Tell Jesus you're sorry for the wrong things you've done, and ask Him to come and make your heart His home.

# IT'S POSSIBLE!

*All things are
possible with God.*

MARK 10:27

"All things" means *all things,* or it doesn't
mean anything. God is not a liar. All His
promises are true. So trust Him. Take Him
at His Word. *All things are possible with God!*

# Everywhere I Go

*You, O Lord, will bless your children*
*and surround them with your favor.*

Psalm 5:12

There's nothing you can do about it, so you might as well get used to it. When your heart belongs to Jesus, His goodness and love will hunt you down and hug you—so tight the only thing you'll be able to say is, "Thank You, Lord!"

# WHO TOUCHED ME?

*Your faith has healed you.*
*Go in peace.*

LUKE 8:48

For twelve years the woman in this story tried everything and everyone she could think of to help her feel better—and none of it helped! But one day she met Jesus. And when she reached out to Him, guess what happened?

# GUARD YOUR HEART

*Above all else guard your heart.*

PROVERBS 4:23

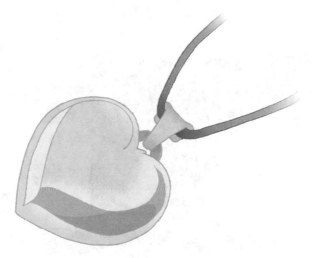

Your heart is God's home. What kind of stuff have you been welcoming inside? Is God's love flowing freely in a clean, pure heart? Or are you allowing a bunch of dirty, stinky feet to track mud all over God's beautiful new house?

# HIDE, SEEK, AND SAVE

*God's Son came to seek
and save what was lost.*

LUKE 19:10

Do you like to play hide-and-seek? Jesus does, too. But He doesn't play fair. He always knows where everyone is hiding! Do you know someone who needs to hear about God's love? Why not find them now and tell them what God can do!

# NOT SO FAST!

*The Lord is slow to get angry
but quick to forgive.*

NUMBERS 14:18

Do you know someone who's quick to get
angry when you've done something wrong?
Not much fun, is it? God is not like that. He
loves to forgive. Did you make a mistake? Tell
God you're sorry. He will wash your sin away.

# HANG IN THERE!

*Those who wait on the Lord
will find new strength.*

ISAIAH 40:31

Don't you know? Haven't you heard? The Lord is God. His love lasts forever! He doesn't get tired. He gives strength to those who are tired! So look up—*and hang on*—help is on the way.

# LIKE AN EAGLE

*Those who wait on the Lord. . .*
*will soar on wings like an eagle.*

ISAIAH 40:31

Have you ever seen an eagle in flight? They circle and climb without moving their wings! How do they do it? It's a little like worship. They spread out their wings and let the wild, warm, wonderful air pull them up toward heaven.

# KEEP ON TRUCKIN'

*Those who wait on the Lord. . .*
*will run and not get tired.*

ISAIAH 40:31

Are your tires bald? Is your engine hot? Are you just about out of gas? Pull over quick! Fill up on God's Word! Don't make the tow truck driver drag you off the road and out of the race.

# ONE MORE MINUTE

*Those who wait on the Lord. . .
will walk and not faint.*

ISAIAH 40:31

Have you ever watched someone fall asleep?
It's kind of funny, isn't it? One minute they're
wide awake, and the next thing you know
their mouth drops open and—*klunk!* It's off to
dreamland. What about you? Are you ready to
get up and go? Or do you need to take a little
more time to curl up in God's lap and rest?

# By His Stripes

*His wounds have healed you.*

1 PETER 2:24

"Just say the word, and my servant will be healed," the soldier said. When Jesus heard this, He was amazed and replied, "I have not found anyone in Israel with such great faith. Go! It will be done just as you believed it would." And the servant was healed at that very hour.

# WHAT'S FOR SUPPER?

*You cannot live on bread alone.*
*Your life must come from*
*the Word of God.*

MATTHEW 4:4

Is your poor little tummy rumbly and grumbly? It's saying, "Feed me. I'm hungry!" Is your heart grumpy, frumpy, and down-in-the-dumpy? It's saying, "Help! I need to hear God's Word!"

# DARE TO DREAM

*Glory to God, who by His mighty power at work within us, is able to do far more than we would dare to ask, hope, or dream.*

EPHESIANS 3:20

Do you have a dream? Place it in God's hands. Let Him shape it as He pleases. He will make it come true—and in a way that is far better than you ever dared to hope, dream, or pray it would.

# Oh Yes, It Is!

*If we claim to be without sin,*
*we are lying to ourselves*
*and the truth is not in us.*

1 John 1:6

Have you ever seen someone with a great, big pimple? There's no way to hide it, is there? Sin is like that. You can say it's not there—but oh, yes it is! Everyone can see it. God sees it, too. So tell Him you're sorry. He will wash *your* sin away.

# READY TO FORGIVE

*Oh LORD, You are good,
full of love and ready to forgive.*

PSALM 86:5

Jesus loves you just the way you are. You don't have to pretend that you haven't done anything wrong. God is not mad at you—He loves you—and He is ready to forgive right now.

# HAND IN HAND

*I will lead them on a level path
where they will not stumble.*

JEREMIAH 31:9

**Where** is Jesus going? Sometimes it's hard to tell. But wherever He leads you, and whatever He asks you to do, you can trust Him. He will always be right there at your side.

# SPLAT—BOOM!

*Pride goes before a fall.*

PROVERBS 16:18

Do you want to fall down and go boom?
It's easy! Just tell yourself you are bigger, better,
smarter, and stronger than everyone else, and
before you know it—*boom*—down you'll go!

# GOOD TO SEE YOU

*Blessed is he who comes
in the name of the Lord.*

PSALM 118:26

Do you know someone who's gloomy and sad?
Bring him good news! Tell him about God's
amazing love. He will be so very glad you came.

# THIS IS THE DAY

*This is the day the Lord has made.*
*I will rejoice and be glad!*

PSALM 118:24

It's another beautiful day today, isn't it? The sun is shining. The air is crisp and cool. The Lord filled it all with incredible things. So tell Him that you love Him. Let Him hear your voice. Fill this good day with thanks and praise!

# ARMED FOR BATTLE

*When the enemy comes in like a flood the Spirit of the Lord will raise the flag for battle and drive him far away.*

ISAIAH 59:19

Are worry and doubt threatening to sweep your faith away? Stand firm. God is with you. His mighty arms will protect you. Trust His promises and watch your enemies melt away.

# SPECIAL GIFTS

*God gave each of you many
special gifts. Use them to serve
one another with love.*

1 PETER 4:10

Did Jesus give you a special gift?
It's time to share it with someone you love.

# LISTEN UP

*Listen to advice, accept instruction,
and you will be wise.*

PROVERBS 19:20

Are you a good listener? I said, *"Are you a good listener?"* Just about everyone loves to talk, talk, talk. But if you're ever going to learn something from someone *you must want to be taught*—or you won't ever learn anything from anyone!

# MUCH TO LEARN

*A foolish man thinks his own way is right.*
*But a wise man listens to others.*

PROVERBS 12:15

Have you noticed that people who think
they are *right about everything* don't ever seem
to be right about *anything*? A wise man knows
he has much to learn and looks for someone
who can teach him!

# SUCCESS

*Plans go wrong when you don't
ask for help, but godly advice
will bring success.*

PROVERBS 15:22

Everyone has something to learn. And
everyone has something to teach someone else.
Take time to listen to friends who love Jesus. And
help when you know Jesus wants you to help.

# FOR ME?

*You love to give good gifts, but your heavenly Father is even more anxious to give good things to all those who ask.*

MATTHEW 7:11

Did you ever give a special gift to someone you love? Do you remember the wonderful feeling you had when you knew they liked it very much? That's how Jesus feels when He gets to do something special for you!

# FISHERS OF MEN

*Come and follow Me and I will make you fishers of men.*

MARK 1:17

Do you like to go fishing? Jesus does, too. But when Jesus goes fishing, He doesn't fish for fish. He fishes for *men!* How do you catch those? You love them so much they don't want to let go!

# PATIENCE PLEASE

*Be patient, trust the LORD. . .*
*and the land will be yours.*

PSALM 37:7, 9

Some things happen very quickly. Others seem to take forever. But if you can learn to wait without worrying or wanting to give up, everything God promised can be yours.

# DON'T GET UPSET

*Don't get upset when the plans of evil men succeed. Trust the LORD and the land will be yours.*

PSALM 37:7, 9

Sometimes it seems like the bad guys always win. But don't get upset. If you trust God and wait, He will make all things—even the bad things—work together for your good.

# No Thank You

*Turn your back on anger and wrath.*
*It only leads to harm.*

PSALM 37:8

Anger never makes *anything* better. The more you feed it, the bigger it grows. When you feel its flames rising up inside, *stop!* Turn and walk away or it will burn your joy down to the ground.

# HAPPY AND FREE

*The wicked plot against the godly. . .but their swords will pierce their own hearts.*

PSALM 37:12, 15

There will be times when people try to hurt you. But don't get discouraged. God sees every heart. He knows every plan. One day the trap they set will snap shut on their own hands. And they will watch you walk away, happy and free.

# SHATTERED

*The power of evil men will be shattered,
but the LORD takes care of the godly.*

PSALM 37:17

Why are there so many mean people in the
world? I just don't know. But I do know this:
Jesus loves each and every one of them. And
we need to do our best to love them, too.

# MONEY, MONEY

*The love of money
is the root of all evil.*

1 TIMOTHY 6:10

Do you love money? If the deep roots of your heart are wound tightly around the riches of this world, sooner or later the fruit on your tree will become rotten. It will poison everyone.

# GET RICH QUICK!

*People who want to get rich fall
into a trap, and do many foolish
things that ruin everything.*

1 TIMOTHY 6:9

Do you like to work hard? God will bless the
things you do, and you will always have enough.
Do you dream of being rich? No matter how
much you get, you will never, ever have enough!

# GOD AND MONEY

*You cannot serve
both God and money.*

MATTHEW 6:24

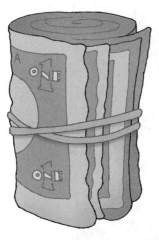

You cannot serve two masters. You will either love one and hate the other, or you will be loyal to one and turn your back on the other. So don't get all upset worrying about money. Put Jesus first, and you will always have everything you need.

# ALL HE PROMISED

*Be patient, do what God says,
and you will receive all He promised.*

HEBREWS 10:36

No one likes to wait. But waiting can be
a blessing. It only becomes a problem when
you look away from Jesus—and begin to fill
your mind with worry, fear, and doubt.

# ONE AND ONLY

*There is only one God, and only one man who can bring us to God, and that man is Jesus.*

1 TIMOTHY 2:5

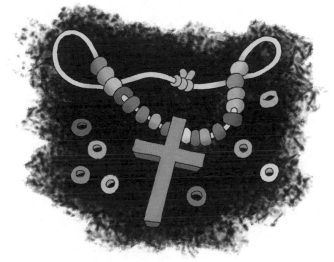

There is only one God. There has never been another. There never will be. The only One who can bring us together—*and the only One who ever could*—is the man, Jesus Christ.

# Right Now

*Don't let anyone look down on you because you are young. Instead be an example in all you say and do.*

1 Timothy 4:12

Your life matters. It matters right now! You don't have to wait until you are older or richer or bigger or smarter. You can be the one who helps God bring the change someone needs *right now*.

# EVERYONE

*Everyone everywhere will be blessed because of you.*

GENESIS 28:14

The wonderful things you do will never be forgotten. God's love has changed your heart. And now your new life is changing everything and everyone around you for good—*forever!*

# BEAR WITH ME

*Bear with each other
and forgive as the Lord forgave you.*

COLOSSIANS 3:13

**Are** you a teddy bear? Or are you a *grizzly bear?*
Or are you sometimes both? Life can get a bit
hairy. So it's always best to forgive and forget.
And a great big bear hug wouldn't hurt either!

# ALL BECAUSE OF YOU

*Honor your father and mother,
and you will live a long, happy life.*

EXODUS 20:12

Your mom or dad take good care of you,
don't they? Just look at how beautiful you are—
*they must!* I'm sure they deserve some kind of
award, don't you think? What can you give them?
How about a helping hand and a thankful heart?

# NEVER THIRSTY AGAIN

*All those who drink the water I give will never be thirsty again.*

JOHN 4:14

A heart without Jesus is like a man lost forever in the desert. The only thing he can think about is how to get another drink. God's Word is the living water that will set a lost heart free. Lead a man to it, and he will never be thirsty again!

# LIVING WATER

*The water I give will become
a fountain overflowing
with eternal life.*

JOHN 4:14

Cool, clear water can satisfy the most terrible thirst. But no matter how much you drink, you will always be thirsty again. The water Jesus gives is living and eternal and fills *everyone* who drinks it with beauty and new life forever.

# MY HIDING PLACE

*You are my hiding place.*
*You will protect me from harm*
*and surround me with songs of victory.*

PSALM 32:7

When the going gets tough, the tough get going! But *where* do you go when the going gets tough? If you are smart, you go to Jesus!

# DAY AND NIGHT

*My heart cries out to You day and night.
How I long to see your face! For when
You come, we will learn to do right.*

ISAIAH 26:9

Jesus, will You come and fill our hearts today?
Fill them with Your goodness and love. Fill them
with the desire to help others. Here are our hands.
Please take them and make something beautiful.

# SEEK THE LORD

*Seek the LORD. He can still be found!*
*Call on Him now! He is near.*

ISAIAH 55:6

When is the best time to spend time with Jesus? In the morning when you first wake up? At night before you go to bed? The best time to spend time with Jesus is *now!*

# You Will Find Him

*If you seek the LORD you will find Him,
when you search for Him with all your heart.*

DEUTERONOMY 4:29

Jesus is not hiding. If you look for Him,
you will find Him. He is always ready to love
you when you seek Him with all your heart.

# THE GREATEST

*The one who humbles himself
like a little child is the greatest
in the kingdom of heaven.*

MATTHEW 18:4

Would you like to become the greatest person
in heaven and earth? It's easier than you think.
When you finally realize you can't do *anything*
without God's help—you are the greatest!

# KNEES AND TOES

*Unless I wash you,
you don't really belong to Me.*

JOHN 13:8

Has anyone ever washed your feet? It makes
you feel kind of funny, doesn't it? Why is it so
hard to let someone do such a simple thing?
Peter didn't want Jesus to wash his feet either.
Why not? Peter knew he was dirty! And once
his dirty foot was in Jesus' hands, there was no
way to hide it. No servant is greater than His
master. But our Master willingly became a servant.
And that's what He wants us to do as well.

# READY TO HELP

*Serve each other with love,*
*for God resists the proud,*
*but He gives help to the humble.*

1 PETER 5:5

Are your hands ready to help someone else?
Then God's hands are always ready to help *you*.

# THANK YOU, JESUS

*Humble yourself before the LORD*
*and He will lift you up.*

JAMES 4:10

It's nice when people notice the good things you do. When you remember to thank God for giving you those special talents and gifts, *He will notice*—and be very pleased as well.

# BEFORE THE SUN SETS

*Don't let the sun go down while you are still angry with your friend, for anger gives the devil a grip on your heart.*

EPHESIANS 4:26–27

Are you angry with someone today? Don't let the devil dig his claws into your heart. Do everything you can to forgive and make things right—before the sun goes down on this day.

# DON'T STEP ON THAT!

*Stay away from angry, hot-tempered people, or you will learn to be like them, and they will capture your heart.*

PROVERBS 22:24–25

Spending a lot of time with a hot-tempered person is like stepping on a skunk. Before you know it, you're covered head to toe—and there's no easy way to get the terrible smell out.

# I Found You

*When you find Me you find life.*

PROVERBS 8:35

Do you ever wait at the door for your daddy to come home? What do you do when you see him coming? Jesus is happy when you spend time together. He will fill your life with every good thing when you come running to Him.

# BE STRONG AND WORK

*Be strong and work, for I am with you.*

HAGGAI 2:4

Do you have a big job to do? Be strong! Trust God to help you, and get to work. Jesus is with you. He has everything you need and will show you what to do—every single step of the way.

# BY MY SPIRIT

*Not by might or by power,
but by My Spirit says the Lord.*

ZECHARIAH 4:6

God's mighty power is yours for the asking. But when you do things your own way, without asking what He wants, you unplug yourself from God's power. The help you need will not flow freely until you get back on your knees.

# SUCH A TIME AS THIS

*You were born
for such a time as this.*

ESTHER 4:14

God made you for a purpose. Your life is important in ways you cannot even imagine. Someone needs to hear what you have to say. So don't hold back. Love God with all your heart. Be everything you were born to be.

# PRESS ON

*I am not perfect. But I press on to make God's perfection my own because He has taken hold of my heart.*

PHILIPPIANS 3:12

Yes, you've made a few mistakes. *But you are forgiven!* Forget the past. Look forward to all that lies ahead. Run the race all the way to the end. Heaven is waiting—and Jesus is there!

# LOVE YOUR NEIGHBOR

*If you love your neighbor
as much as you love yourself,
you are doing right.*

JAMES 2:8

Just think how much better most things
would be if we would simply learn how to love
other people the way we want them to love us!

# NOBODY'S PERFECT

*The Lord disciplines those He loves.*

## HEBREWS 12:6

Even good apples have a few brown spots, right? After all, nobody's perfect. So why doesn't Jesus overlook *our* rotten, mushy parts? Because He loves us way too much to leave us that way!

# BEAUTIFUL AND ALIVE

*My Word will not return empty.*

ISAIAH 55:11

God's promises are powerful and alive. Like rain that falls to water the earth, when God's Word is spoken, He makes everything bloom and grow just the way it should.

# ALL THE TIME

*God is light.*
*There is no darkness in Him.*

1 JOHN 1:5

God is good all the time! When you ask Him to come and live in your heart, His love will shine like a blinding light—driving every last little bit of darkness out once and for all.

# Not Just a Gift

*God is love.*

1 John 4:8

Love is not just a gift God gives. And it's not simply something He does or will do. It's much more than something He longs to give to you. Love is alive. It's what God is!

# ALIVE IN OUR HEARTS

*If we love one another, God lives in us,
and His love is truly alive in our hearts*

1 JOHN 4:12

Some people are easy to love. And others
are not! When you do your best to love without
making fun or finding fault, everyone will know
Jesus is alive in your heart.

# I'll Say It Again

*Again I tell you, if two of you agree about anything you ask for, it will be done for you by My Father in heaven.*

MATTHEW 18:19

Unity is a powerful thing. When the hearts of two believers join together and pray as one, there's no telling what amazing things God will do!

# TWO OR THREE

*When two or three of you
come together in My name,
I am there with you.*

MATTHEW 18:20

Jesus always hears you when you pray. But
when you join hearts and minds with others
and begin to cry out as one, Jesus says He will
be right there in the middle of it with you.

# Barbecued!

*If you enemy is hungry, feed him.
If he's thirsty, give him a drink—and
the Lord will reward you.*

PROVERBS 25:21–22

When you do something nice for someone who has been mean to you, Jesus says it's like dumping a bucket of hot coals on his head. Your kindness will teach a lesson that cannot be missed—and God will reward you for it.

# EVEN A CHILD

*Even a child is known
by his actions.*

PROVERBS 20:11

What you do and where you go say a lot
about who you are. Your kind and gentle heart
makes a world of difference to everyone around
you—even those who make fun of you for it.

# ONLY ONE

*There is a way that seems right
to a man, but in the end
it only leads to death.*

PROVERBS 14:12

God's way is the only right way. Some
folks don't want to hear that, but it's true.
Yes, you can take any road you please. They
all lead somewhere. A few lead nowhere.
But only *one* will lead you to heaven.

# A PROMISE FOREVER

*Heaven and earth will pass away, but My promises will last forever.*

MATTHEW 24:35

God's promises are yours forever. Nothing can ever take them away. So hold on to them tightly. Trust them with all your heart. They are the greatest treasure you will ever own.

# BENT OUT OF SHAPE

*Do not let your heart be troubled.*
*Trust in God, and trust in Me.*

JOHN 14:1

Has someone been rattling your cage?
Do they have you all bent out of shape? Stop
listening to all their noise, noise, noise, noise!
Let Jesus come and quiet your heart.

# MY FATHER'S HOUSE

*My Father's house has many rooms.
I am going there now to prepare
a place just for you.*

JOHN 14:2

Death is not really the end of anything.
It's the beginning of everything! Jesus will take
care of you *all your life*. And when it's time to
step out of this world, He will be there to make
sure you get to your new home safely as well.

# THE KINGDOM OF HEAVEN

*Let the little children come to Me,
for the kingdom of heaven
belongs to them.*

MARK 10:14

Is God's love alive deep inside your heart?
Then everything Jesus has is yours. You're never
too small or too young. You can come to Jesus
all by yourself. God's love is *yours*. When you
ask, He will give *you* everything you need.

# EVERY KNEE WILL BOW

*At the name of Jesus every knee will bow and every tongue will openly declare that He is the Lord.*

PHILIPPIANS 2:10–11

Would you like to see Jesus face-to-face? One day everyone will bow down before Him. And on that day, the people who made fun of you for trusting Him and believing His promises will find out what you have known all along: *Jesus is the King of everyone and everything!*

# GOOD HANDS

*I trust in you, O LORD. You are my God.*
*My times are in Your hands.*

PSALM 31:14–15

Jesus loves you. He knows what you need today. He knows what you will need tomorrow. You can relax and enjoy this good day. Your life is in good hands—*your life is in God's hands!*

# NOT ASHAMED

*I am not ashamed of the good news about Jesus Christ. It has the power to save everyone who believes.*

ROMANS 1:16

It can be a little scary to tell someone about Jesus and the way He will come into your heart. But remember, God's Word will save *everyone* who believes. So don't hold back. On the outside, people may think you're crazy. But deep inside they are asking, "Why did I wait so long?"

# UNDER HIS FEET

*God put everything under His feet,
making Him the head of everything for
the good of all His children everywhere.*

EPHESIANS 1:22

Jesus' name stands above every other name.
Nothing has any power over Him. No man can
tell Him where to go or what to do. Everything
He has belongs to you as well. So talk to Him
today. Let Him show you what love can do.

# SOFT AND STRETCHY

*No one pours new wine into old skins. If he does, the skins will burst, and both the wine and the skins will be ruined.*

MARK 2:22

Are you soft and stretchy? Or are you dry and crusty? Jesus wants to pour something new and exciting into your life. Are you flexible enough to receive it? Or are you so set in your ways that God will have to give it all to someone else?

# FILLED!

*Every wine skin
should be filled with wine.*

JEREMIAH 13:12

Change can be hard. Some folks like things the way they are. There's nothing wrong with that, as long as God is there. But young or old, Jesus wants all of His children to be filled with the new life that only His Spirit can bring.

# MILK AND HONEY

*The LORD your God
is bringing you into a good land.*

DEUTERONOMY 8:7

Do you like good things? That's good! When you follow Jesus, you won't always know where you are going. But you can know this: When you get there, it will definitely be good!

# FOLLOW THE LEADER

*Be strong! Believe in the Lord
and trust His mighty power.*

EPHESIANS 6:10

Jesus said the land He is leading you to will
be good. But He never said it would be easy to
get there! So be strong. Trust His mighty power
and follow Him wherever He wants you to go.

# LOOK AT THAT!

*The man who never stops looking at, living out, and believing God's promises will be blessed in all he does.*

JAMES 1:25

It's good to hear what God says. And it's even better to believe it. But when you hear what God says, believe what God says, and then *do* what God says, He will bless everything you do.

# SERVE SOMEBODY

*Serve one another, as if you were serving the LORD, for He will reward everyone for the good they do.*

EPHESIANS 6:7–8

Would you like to give just about everyone a really big surprise they'll never forget? Give them the one gift they've probably never seen before. Treat them with kindness and respect!

# In It to Win It

*Throw out everything that gets in your way and run the race Jesus set before you with all of your might.*

Hebrews 12:1

**If** you were in a race and you wanted to win, what would you do? Strap an elephant to your back? Fill your pants with cement? Glue your shoes to the floor? Of course not! Don't ever let worry, fear, and doubt keep you out of the race. Throw them off and run with all your might!

# GOTCHA!

*Stop doing wrong things!*
*Let God's Spirit help you put them*
*to death and you will live as He desires.*

ROMANS 8:13

Sin moves out when Jesus moves in. But every now and then a few rats will try to sneak back into the house. Don't let them nibble a bunch of holes into all the good things God has done. Kill them quick—or they will chew up everything!

# I WILL ANSWER

*Call to Me and I will answer you and
tell you great and mighty things you
could never understand on your own.*

JEREMIAH 33:3

Do you have a lot of BIG questions? Jesus has
a lot of big answers! Your questions don't bother
Him. They make Him happy. So call Him up.
Tell Him how you feel. Jesus hears you. He will
answer. But first you've got to *call Him up!*

# FAITHFUL AND TRUE

*The Lord will keep His promise of love to a thousand generations of those who love Him and keep His commands.*

DEUTERONOMY 7:9

God's love is a promise He will keep *forever*. Nothing will *ever* make Him change His mind or turn His back on *anyone* who loves Him, who does what He says.

# EVERYONE WHO CALLS

*Everyone who calls
on the Lord will be saved.*

JOEL 2:32

Would you like Jesus to come into your heart? If you ask Him, *He will come!* It doesn't matter who you are. It doesn't matter what you've done. *Everyone* who asks will be saved.

# Just for You

*Unto us a child is born.*
*Unto us a son is given.*

Isaiah 9:6

**Christmas** is coming. Are you ready? God has something very special picked out just for you. In fact, your present has been wrapped and waiting for over two thousand years.

# THE GIFT

*He will be called Wonderful, Counselor, Mighty God, Everlasting Father, Prince of Peace.*

ISAIAH 9:6

What could be inside God's special Christmas gift? Let me give you a hint! His gift will show you the way when you don't know what to do. It will supply you with *everything* you need— *forever!* Its awesome power and the joy it brings will never run dry. And it will fill *everything it touches* with wonderful peace. What could it be? You have to open it to find out. But I'm certain you will never, ever find another gift like it!

# GOD WITH US

*The LORD will give you a sign. The virgin
will bear a child. She will give birth to
a son, and they will call him Immanuel.*

ISAIAH 7:14

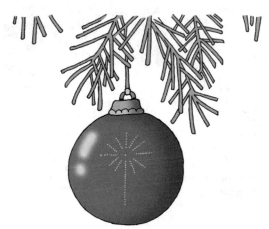

That's right. *God's gift is Jesus!* God chose
to be with us by becoming a child. And because
He did, now we can be with Him. When you
make room for Jesus inside your heart, He will
be born in you—and you will be born again.

# JUST WAIT AND SEE!

*Be patient. Stand firm.*
*The Lord is coming soon.*

JAMES 5:8

It's hard to wait, isn't it? Especially when you know something good is coming very soon. Waiting without worry is a sign of real faith. It's like shouting, "God always keeps His promises. Just you wait and see!"

# HOME AGAIN

*I will come back and take you with Me
so you can be where I am.*

JOHN 14:3

God's house is a big, BIG house.
He has a special room waiting there just for
you. One day Jesus will come again. You will
put your hand in His and together you will
step out of this world and into heaven *forever!*

# ABRAHAM

*Abraham never doubted, and he never stopped believing. He knew God would do what He said He would do.*

ROMANS 4:19–21

Abraham was an old, old man—almost one hundred years old! But he believed God would always keep His promises. And because Abraham believed, that's exactly what God did!

# BLESSED OR STRESSED?

*Come back to Me.*
*Trust Me and rest and you will be safe.*

ISAIAH 30:15

How was your day? Was it wild and crazy? Are you ready to pop? Did you bounce off the walls? Or did you take time to *stop*. . .set all the busy things aside. . .and let God fill your heart with peace so you'd be blessed and not stressed?

# SILENT NIGHT

*May the Lord of Peace give you peace
at all times and in every way.*

2 THESSALONIANS 3:16

Are you having a silent, holy night? Or are you tearing your hair out in fuzzy brown clumps? Why not put everything down and rest? Let God's peace flow over you like the cool air on a winter morning. Christmas is coming. Are you ready?

# O BETHLEHEM

*O Bethlehem, even though
you are small, the shepherd and ruler
of all Israel will come from you.*

MICAH 5:2

Jesus was not born in a palace. He was born in a manger. He was not born among kings. He was born among poor shepherds. Why? What was He trying to tell us? What did He want us to know?

# CHRISTMAS

*Today in the city of David*
*your savior is born;*
*He is Christ the Lord.*

LUKE 2:11

Christmas is here. Your savior is born!
It's not a just another story. It's real and it's true.
So hurry! Open the gift God picked out just for
you. Let Jesus be born in your heart today.

# CLOSE TO HIS HEART

*He cares for His flock like a shepherd.
He gathers His lambs up in His arms
and holds them close to His heart.*

ISAIAH 40:11

You are Jesus' precious little lamb. He watches over you day and night. Have you wandered off into the dark? Run back home just as fast as you can! Let the Shepherd scoop you up in His mighty arms—and hold you close to His heart.

# WHERE ARE MY KEYS?

*I asked the Lord for help, and He helped
Me and set me free from all my fears.*

PSALM 34:4

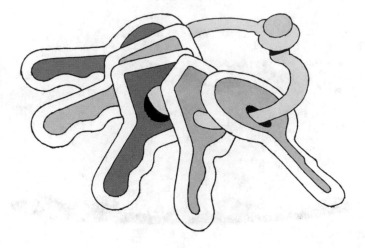

Fear is a prison. It will lock you up behind icy
fingers and keep God's promises just out of reach.
But fear not! Faith is the key that will open the
lock and set you free. So where are *your* keys?

# STEADY NOW!

*The LORD is my strength. He makes my feet steady and helps me to stand.*

HABAKKUK 3:19

Ooops! Watch out! Are you starting to slip? Trust God. Believe His promises. They will always be steady ground beneath your feet.

# LEARN AND LIVE

*No discipline is pleasant. But a harvest of peace is waiting for all those who allow themselves to be trained by it.*

HEBREWS 12:11

Do you love Jesus? Then you must allow Him to correct you when you are wrong. Have you wandered down the wrong road? It's not too late to turn around. He will let you start over. But you must listen when you hear Him whisper, *"Stop!"*

# WAITING FOR YOU THERE

*The LORD will go before you,
protecting you from all that lies ahead
and everything that has gone behind.*

ISAIAH 52:12

It's been a good year in every way. But this good year will soon be gone. A brand-new year is about to begin. What all lies ahead? No one knows for sure. But wherever you go and whatever you do, you can always know this: *God is good and Jesus is already waiting for you there!*

# INDEX

**GOD'S FAITHFULNESS** Day 121, 133, 136, 155, 164, 165, 175, 183, 186, 187, 199, 200, 201, 202, 203, 217, 221, 225, 233, 236, 242, 246, 247, 249, 251, 252, 253, 257, 297, 298, 328, 334, 337, 348, 349, 354, 365

**GOD'S GOODNESS** Day 3, 73, 74, 75, 106, 133, 136, 138, 139, 153, 160, 161, 163, 165, 181, 190, 192, 198, 199, 206, 213, 221, 228, 234, 236, 237, 238, 245, 246, 247, 249, 265, 324, 340, 341

**GOD'S LOVE** Day 1, 10, 11, 15, 19, 22, 23, 28, 29, 39, 40, 41, 43, 46, 48, 52, 53, 54, 65, 66, 69, 71, 78, 83, 93, 94, 96, 97, 98, 100, 111, 121, 122, 135, 136, 139, 155, 156, 157, 158, 159, 160, 162, 163, 166, 171, 178, 181, 183, 186, 188, 198, 206, 219, 225, 234, 235, 246, 247, 258, 266, 288, 322, 325, 334, 335, 337, 349, 351, 355, 361, 365

**GOD'S POWER** Day 23, 33, 59, 89, 96, 97, 99, 108, 109, 135, 182, 188, 235, 236, 256, 260, 276, 306, 323, 336, 339

# WRITE TO PHIL A. SMOUSE!

Once upon a time, Phil A. Smouse wanted to be a scientist. But scientists don't get wonderful letters and pictures from friends like you. So Phil decided to draw and color instead! He and his wife live in southwestern Pennsylvania. They have two children they love with all their heart.

Phil loves to tell kids like you all about Jesus. He would love to hear from you today! So get out your markers and crayons and send a letter or a picture to:

Phil A. Smouse
Barbour Publishing, Inc.
1810 Barbour Drive
Uhrichsville, OH 44683

Or visit his website at www.philsmouse.com/
and send him an e-mail at: phil@philsmouse.com.